Wheel of Fortune

Getting to the Heart of Business Strategy

BOB EMILIANI
MASSIMO TORINESI

Wheel of Fortune / Bob Emiliani and Massimo Torinesi

Cover design by Bob Emiliani.

ISBN-13: 978-1-7320191-4-0
Library of Congress Control Number: 2021900080

1. Business 2. Strategy 3. Leadership

First Edition: January 2021

Published by Cubic LLC, South Kingstown, Rhode Island, USA. ⚓

This publication is believed to provide accurate information with respect to the subject matter covered. It is sold with the understanding that it does not in any way represent legal, financial, business, consulting, or other professional service.

Manufactured using digital print-on-demand technology.

CONTENTS

"It is mind alone that perceives that
competition is wasteful"

— Lester F. Ward (1841-1913)

About the Cover

In medieval and ancient philosophy, the Wheel of Fortune, or *Rota Fortunae*, is a symbol of the capricious nature of Fate. The wheel belongs to the goddess Fortuna (Greek equivalent Tyche) who spins it at random, changing the positions of those on the wheel: some suffer great misfortune, others gain windfalls. The metaphor was already a cliché in ancient times, complained about by Tacitus, but was greatly popularized for the Middle Ages by its extended treatment in the Consolation of Philosophy by Boethius from around 520. It became a common image in manuscripts of the book, and then other media, where Fortuna, often blindfolded, turns a large wheel of the sort used in watermills, to which kings and other powerful figures are attached.

The Wheel was widely used as an allegory in medieval literature and art to aid religious instruction. Though classically Fortune's Wheel could be favorable and disadvantageous, medieval writers preferred to concentrate on the tragic aspect, dwelling on downfall of the mighty – serving to remind people of the temporality of earthly things.

– Source: Wikipedia

Preface

Business strategy is just something you do as the leader of a company, right? It is both a requirement and an obligation. It embodies a multitude of values drawn from diverse areas such as business, economics, finance, leadership, management, and society. These values both form the need for strategy and determine its shape and substance. As such, business strategy reflects what leaders think they must do and why. Leaders of businesses of all sizes, from mom-and-pop to the largest multinational corporations develop strategies and work to put them into action. Business strategy can be informal, the whim of the small business owner, or it can be highly formalized by the leadership team and board of directors. Either way it points toward goals and objectives that must be maintained or achieved to assure success and prosperity.

Regardless of whether it is achieved, the strategy will be superseded by a new or modified strategy destined in due time to be replaced again and again for as long as the business exists. This process of concatenating strategies is facilitated by both turnover in top leadership and changes in market conditions as time passes. The varied strategies give the impression of attentiveness to changing business conditions and changing opinions of what is necessary to be successful in the future. But mostly, it is a cycling through of common strategies, used singularly or in combination to achieve one particular end. As such, strategy development and execution lack imagination and creativity, and its benefits, when realized, are usually narrow in scope.

This is not the usual book about business strategy. It seeks to challenge leaders' understanding of strategy and its utility in relation to success and prosperity. We question conventional wisdom, the preconceptions that leaders have about strategy. In doing so, our objective is to analyze the basis for formulating strategy and the limitations created by business strategy. We do this from novel perspectives: business and social theories of strategy. In our use of the word "theory," we intend it as a practical explanation for existential phenomena – that which exists in the so-called "real world." In developing these explanations, we reveal great weakness in strategy development and execution that others do not recognize or dismiss as irrelevant. Additionally, we show how business strategy, as well as its focused execution, narrows choices and limits the human creativity and imagination necessary for business success and prosperity. As such, strategy reflects constraint, rather than freedom, which often results in embarrassing and expensive corporate failures.

We also carefully examine a major business strategy failure, the Boeing 737 Max, using a novel method of analysis designed to pinpoint the problems in executive thinking and decision-making. The failure analysis method informs readers of structural weaknesses that exist in strategy development and execution which must be corrected. We also present a new method for avoiding future failures by applying simple tests to current or proposed strategies evaluated against various causative criteria.

From this analysis of strategy failure, we hope to move

readers from the common reflexive approaches to problem-solving, wherein strategy consists primarily of copying what other leaders do, to higher levels of imagination and creativity. To move into the realm of new ideas, combinations of new ideas, and unconstrained imagination, with an acute awareness of how and why strategies fail.

We hope this volume gives leaders much to reflect on and motivates them to rethink strategy and propel them towards designing combinations of productive methods that result in improved organizational functionality and resultant favorable outcomes. It gives readers both the rationale and permission to think differently about both strategy and execution, as well as leaders' roles and responsibilities. We hope that leaders take a great interest in analyzing strategy failures and avoiding future failures using the new methods presented here.

Bob Emiliani
South Kingstown, Rhode Island

Massimo Torinesi
Milan, Italy
January 2021

Introduction

The understanding of business depends upon one's role in a business. At one end are workers whose understanding of business relates narrowly to their job function of performing one or more tasks in a longer sequence of tasks necessary to produce a product or service. As such, the worker's job is to satisfy an internal or external customer in the required quality and quantity at the required time. This is the detail work of value creation.

At the other end are senior leaders, led by the president or CEO and CFO. Their interest and role is to tend to the pecuniary ends of business. They are essentially property managers (traders in property rights) whose concerns are revenue and cost, acquisition and divestment, debt and leverage, cash flow and stock price, making and receiving payments, shareholders and creditors, and the like. These pecuniary ends are represented by various financial and non-financial metrics or key performance indicators (KPIs). Depending on the size of the business, the pecuniary ends of business can consume little of the CEOs time for small and mid-size businesses or it can be nearly all-consuming for CEOs of large, highly leveraged corporations. In the latter case, the pecuniary ends of business are a type of specialized job function that excludes any concern about the detail work of value creation and interconnected processes performed by workers.

In between the workers and the top leaders are the managers whose job it is to mediate between workers and senior leaders to achieve required corporate goals and objectives. Their job is to react to varied problems that impair functional performance and the overall drive to achieve the pecuniary ends of business. Each does their work according to a set of values associated with the work that stand in relation to both one's position in the hierarchy and the technical demands of the job.

The workers do the intellectual work while senior leaders do the pecuniary work. The former involves facts and causal sequence of processes while the latter involves machinations to increase the value of the property based on the business doctrine of force and fraud, where "force" means mandatory, compulsory, or coercive and "fraud" means non-criminal deceit and trickery. None of this is to say this is wholly unnecessary or incorrect. Nor does it deprecate anyone personally or in their capacity as senior leader. It merely states, in plain terms, the common way that business affairs are understood and practiced, and how they manifest themselves in strategy development and execution. Select leaders are drawn to this pecuniary ambition while the mass of employees is drawn to internal or external customers as the satisficing aspect of business enterprise.

In large companies, employee surveys often show that most employees do not understand the strategy. Efforts are made by leaders to communicate the strategy more often and in complementary ways, yet subsequent employee surveys produce similar results. Leaders' effort to formulate strategy do not resonate with most employees and, therefore, the participation necessary to realize the strategy is limited or suffers from errors that slow the pace of execution. The difference in understanding is because employees, engaged in productive work, have difficulty understanding strategies that are fundamentally nonproductive in their principal design for achieving the narrow goal of pecuniary gain. Business strategy rooted in force and fraud (anticompetitive practice) is a plan for conquest and exploit that seeks to gain "something for nothing;" something in sense of pecuniary gain, nothing in the sense of betterment of productive work processes and methods to satisfy customers.

Additionally, there is often a disconnect between the strategy as written on paper and the methods needed to execute the strategy in practice. The "what" is easy to create, while the "how" is difficult and often delegated to an implementation team. Such teams must develop processes or methods to execute the strategy and generally are not adept at doing so. It is akin to the familiar hand-off between design and manufacturing, which is laden with problems even though manufacturing teams are adept at developing processes. Strategy existing on paper – a blueprint – is nothing more than a wish. If it cannot be executed – manufactured – it is a bad strategy.

Creating business strategy can be a self-evident truth of its importance and worth, but it cannot be accounted for as "real work." It is nonproductive. The real work is in strategy execution. The lack of executive engagement in strategy execution, much like the lack of designer engagement in manufacturing or architect engagement in construction, spells impending trouble. Worse than that is the dismissal of problems that arise in strategy execution, as these are the early warning signs of possible failure. Both represent the common unwillingness among senior leaders to get their hands dirty.

Because of these and other difficulties, strategy is often outsourced to other people and organizations – global management consulting firms, accounting firms, and law firms – to facilitate strategy formulation and execution of strategic moves such as mergers, acquisitions, and divestitures. The danger in outsourcing this work is that these people and organizations do the same work for one's competitors. The possibilities of losing control of proprietary information and being outflanked by one's competitors is real.

Suffice it to say that much has been written about business strategy formulation and execution and the roles and responsibilities of senior leaders in both. One thing is clear, more time should be spent on actual building than on creating paper plans. The value of the former is much greater than the latter. To that end, senior leaders must accept, in some greater measure than is typically the case, the need to get their hands dirty every day, for at least some part of the day, as strategy execution proceeds.

We will present the case that business strategy is a minefield of problems, and, conversely, less a source of solutions to business problems, whose actual value is more limited than is normally realized. This is not to say that business strategy is useless or that senior leaders should not bother with it.

Rather, it means that strategy should be less prominent in executive thinking and be better balanced with individual and organizational capability- and skills-building to adapt to ever-changing (meaning, daily) business conditions.

Is a three- or five-year strategic plan, a defensive strategy, necessary? Perhaps it is. But might there be a need to reverse course and go on offense at some point during that five-year period? What about the reverse case? What is the likelihood that the plan will either need to change or, if stubbornly adhered to, will not come to fruition – or, the plan does come to fruition and leaves the company in worse shape? Isn't the true nature of business to respond to problems as they arise, that leaders accept envelopment in the short- and mid-term range of business exigencies? If so, the greater need is to be able to quickly shift course as circumstances change. The source of competitive advantage comes less from strategy and more from attunement and rapid response to current conditions – the things that everyone, leaders included, need to focus on and get done in the next 30 to 60 days, adaptively, as conditions change. While leaders cannot be overtaken by execution, they likewise must not be blinded by the brilliance of their own business strategy whose details of execution are usually lacking.

A lot can change in the time it takes to create a business strategy or execute the strategy. Focusing on this takes leaders' eyes off what is changing around them. Plans, developed by leaders and rigidly enforced, as is often required, can be like a straitjacket and produce increasingly greater competitive disadvantage as time passes. Leaders' reluctance to change or modify plans stems from an incontrovertible requirement to avoid admitting error or showing weakness in strategic planning or execution. Circumstances such as these introduce gambling-like risk in strategy development and execution, thus greatly lowering the odds of success.

The title of this book is *Wheel of Fortune*. We chose this title because of the risks inherent to strategy development and execution under the social conditions commonly found in organizations of all sizes; social conditions imposed by senior leaders based on their own peculiar wants and needs. For this reason, we contend that the risk of failure is much greater than is commonly realized, and that amelioration of risk is only possible when social conditions commonly found in companies change. We characterize the social condition and provide the justification for change which we hope leaders will accept and act upon accordingly.

Furthermore, business leaders invariably copy one another. If one influential leader thinks they need something to improve business performance, then most other leaders unquestioningly follow suit. This happens in the short-term with new management fads and trends and over the long-term with respect to business strategy. Our leaders scolded us for copying others and forcefully challenged us by asking:

- "Why do you listen to people without thinking?"
- "They said you needed that. You believed them?"
- "How do you know what they said is true?"

- "You must think for yourself."

We have learned through our business experiences to question things generally, and specifically to question what we think we need to achieve a goal or objective. We were challenged to problem-solve at a much higher level than merely copying what other people did. Time and time again we found that we did not need what we thought we needed. We found, individually or in collaboration with others, imaginative and creative ways to solve problems and what needed to be done – usually more quickly and with less resources.

Copying extends to the domain of explanations for strategy failure. It is commonly attributed to reasons such as [1]:

- Poor communication
- Ambiguous or conflicting goals
- Unclear priorities
- Silo behavior
- Wrong culture
- Resistance to change
- Complexity
- Lack of middle management support
- Poor leadership

These simplistic explanations are unsatisfactory and do not get to the core of the problem. We provide a much deeper analysis, one which points to corrective actions that are much more practical, specific, and actionable.

Wheel of Fortune is intended to compel leaders to think. It is a warning against complacency and to avoid the copy-and-paste mentality that has long been common in business. It is a book about developing a better way of thinking and better mental models, because the mind is the foundation for building something better than what currently exists. In today's world, we need more good thinking, imagination, and creativity.

Instead of searching for easy answers, we must ask better questions. Think deeply and imagine freely to create a better future. By thinking differently, leaders can extinguish the common problems and repetitive modes of failure that other organizations experience. We hope this book inspires current and future business leaders to think differently about strategy and strategy execution, and to be more creative and imaginative in relation to the ever-changing needs of customers and the experiences that they desire.

Finally, consider completing the worksheets contained in the final pages of the book (pp. 131-140). Fill them out as you compete reading each section of the book. It will improve your learning and retention, and help remind you of key learnings to share with your colleagues.

References

[1] Kraaijenbrink, J. (2019), "20 Reasons Why Strategy Execution Fails," *Forbes*, 10 September, accessed 31 December 2020, https://www.forbes.com/sites/jeroen kraaijenbrink/2019/09/10/20-reasons-why-strategy-executi on-fails/

1
Business and Strategy

Business and Strategy

Business strategy is a plan to meet a business objective; to solve one or more business problems. The business objective usually pertains to the ends of business which are pecuniary – having to do with money-gain or wealth accumulation. Thus, to be precise, business strategy is a pecuniary strategy, to own more property in one form or another. Strategy is speculative in nature and thus a gamble whose payoff is directed more towards the business than anything or anyone else external to the company. The strategy must result in beneficial outcomes as depicted by an income statement, balance sheet, cash flow statement, and shareholder's equity. Concern about the goods or services sold in terms of their workmanship, quality, process efficiency, etc., is largely the domain of people lower in the hierarchy. In most cases, leadership assumes that what should be happening is, in fact, happening. With this assumption, they can focus on corporate pecuniary strategy to achieve the pecuniary ends of business.

Strategy reflects the transient business interests of senior leaders, owners, and passive investors. It necessarily is a plan to disturb the competitive field of business such that varied forms of gain can be achieved. Most notably, an increase in the amount of property – that which can be possessed, sold, or traded – tangible property such as money or stock and intangible property such as patents, trademarks, or market-share. It is in disequilibrium, chaos, derangement, or dissension that opportunities for gain exist, whether to obstruct, facilitate, or gain control, as the case may be. The aim is to put others at a disadvantage, whether the market is competitive or not, to sabotage [1] (see Note 1) one or more competitors so that one's strategy prevails – at least for a time until something changes.

The intended or preferred outcome, of course, is zero-sum; to gain at the expense of someone else, through buying, selling, or somehow obstructing other businesses. These are the usual actions prescribed by classical and neoclassical economics and which are unequivocally taken to produce what society wants and is thus beneficial to its collective interests. These salutary outcomes are secondary to the overarching requirement for pecuniary gain that business strategy seeks achieve – and to gain as much as possible as quickly as possible with the least effort but not necessarily the lowest cost.

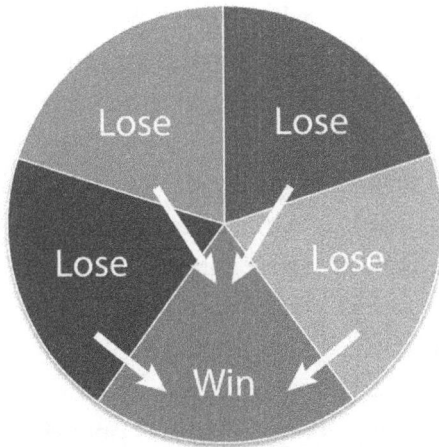

Figure 1-1. The fundamental design of business strategy is for the company to win at the expense of others such as employees, suppliers, customers, and competitors.

What is the purpose of business strategy? Is it to sell more products and services, or is its primary design to increase the value of securities? These can seem to be complementary, yet the former could be aimed towards increasing the sale of goods and services that are not useful or that customers do not need. If so, the strategy impersonalizes customers as an undifferentiable heap of cash to access and secure for one's own benefit – chiefly, the company, top executives (strategists), and shareholders.

Invariably, business strategy, particularly that of mid-size and large corporations, but by no means excluding small businesses, seeks to move away from competition and towards monopoly or similar forms of anticompetitive practice (see Note 2) to disadvantage competitors and gain the upper hand in trade with customers and suppliers and collect the associated pecuniary rewards. The active leadership that exists when faced with competition gives way to a state of indolent leadership fueled by an appetite to avoid competition. Moving in the direction towards monopoly can be satisfying for a time, both personally and in relation to sales and profit growth, but doing so takes leaders towards restful complacency and instills in them and others an inability to compete when marketplace competition eventually returns (Figure 1-2), as it always does (see Note 3). Advantages, whether in intellectual property, products, or services, recede sooner or later. Strategy is an ephemeral pathway to conquest for pecuniary gains and thus gains in the amount of something owned.

So today, as in the past and surely in the future, "being

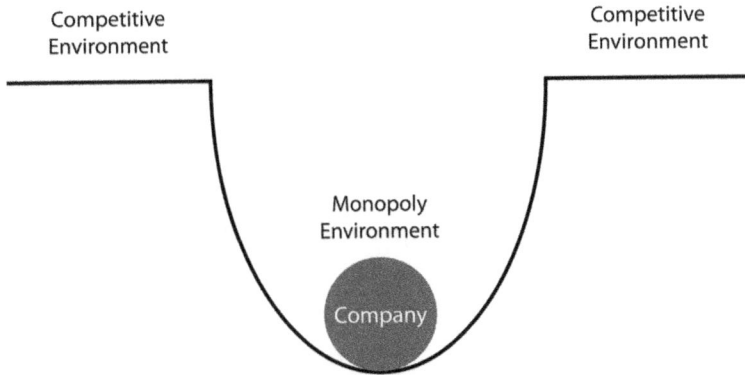

Figure 1-2. Nestled in a state of comfortable rest, the company and its leaders lose their competitive strength and vitality.

strategic" or having a "strategic mindset" means to possess the specialized knowledge and skills necessary to produce pecuniary gains in a quantity and at a rate that meets or exceeds the needs or expectations of owners and investors. It means to acquire as much of the market as possible, in ways that are either friendly or hostile, to "drive the business."

There is a spiritual aspect to strategy, one that is more familiar in terms of conquest than survival. Greater control of the marketplace is seen to be preferred over competitive markets that cannot be easily controlled. There is a satisfaction that comes from taming unruly competitive markets. When such a condition is achieved, one is said to "own the market." With ownership of this intangible property – the marketplace of particular interest – comes the right to do with it as one pleases. It is owned by the company, and its chief, for as long as one can own it, the CEO replicating the royal habit of neutralizing threats and being in control, whether it is real or illusory, durable or temporary.

Humans evolved from a communal society sharing resources to assure survival to an individualistic society where in ownership of property became the distinguishing feature of one's prowess. People feel a need to own things whether in their personal life or in business, and whether it is tangible or intangible. Stewardship is usually not good enough or satisfying enough. The more one owns and controls, the better. The sense of control that comes from ownership of property confers correctness in nearly all thought and action. These elevate one to a higher, more respected status in society. Seen from the opposite direction, there is an expectation that people with high status should own more, control more, know more, and possess answers to life's most vexing questions.

In Western moral philosophy, ownership is a Natural Right. So regardless of government restrictions to prevent monopoly control of markets or industries, business leaders, aided at times by their political allies, will always seek to "own the market" and retain the freedom to do with the property as they please – the individual right secured by Natural Liberty. The labor of the CEO (and CFO) to "own the market" confers a right of property which must be vigorously defended against government incursion. Labor expended to "own the market" means "ownership of the market," as God intended according to Natural Rights.

This is a rogue concept in present day application, having

been born in the Middle Ages during the time of hand craftsmanship and petty trade, not the era of so-called "big business" that emerged in the late 19th century. Nevertheless, the habit of thought established in medieval times, and in some ways much earlier, remains with us today as an unbroken tradition among those who lead. Corporations, legally constructed in ancient times as persons ("corporate personhood"), can own intangible things such as a market, a product of its workman-like labor as embodied by the leader. The march toward monopoly assures brisk business and the avoidance of severe consequences during downturns, to achieve a better rate of return on investment over time than could otherwise be achieved. The question, always, is how much money (profit) can be made doing Option 1 compared to Option 2 or Option 3? Option 1, a march toward monopoly, is the universally favored choice among business leaders. It is the Natural choice seen, fundamentally and eternally, as both right and good.

According to billionaire entrepreneur and venture capitalist, Peter Andreas Thiel [2], "competition is for losers." Mr. Thiel efficiently explains it this way:

"The airlines compete with each other, but Google stands alone. Economists use two simplified models to explain the difference: perfect competition and monopoly. 'Perfect competition' is considered both the ideal and the default state in Economics 101. So-called perfectly competitive markets achieve equilibrium when producer supply meets consumer demand. Every firm in a competitive market is undifferentiated and sells the same homogeneous products. Since no firm has any market power, they must all sell at whatever price the market determines. If there is money to be made, new firms will enter the market, increase supply, drive prices down and thereby eliminate the profits that attracted them in the first place. If too many firms enter the market, they'll suffer losses, some will fold, and prices will rise back to sustainable levels. Under perfect competition, in the long run no company makes an economic profit. The opposite of perfect competition is monopoly. Whereas a competitive firm must sell at the market price, a monopoly owns its market, so it can set its own prices. Since it has no competition, it produces at the quantity and price combination that maximizes its profits... Capitalism is premised on the accumulation of capital, but under perfect competition, all profits get competed away. The lesson for entrepreneurs is clear: If you want to create and capture lasting value, don't build an undifferentiated commodity business... In the real world outside economic theory, every business is successful exactly to the extent that it does something others cannot. Monopoly is therefore not a pathology or an exception. Monopoly is the condition of every successful business."

This, of course, is not an isolated view (see Note 4). Rather, it accurately reflects the spoken, and more often unspoken, view of top business leaders. The questions are (see Note 5): "How do you do it?" and "How far can we go?" What are the knowledge and skills necessary to move away from competition and towards monopoly? Fortunately, prior generations of business leaders figured out the answers to this common problem, as shown in Table 1-1 [3].

This playbook, with most items being long-established and some being more recent, shows that there is little original thinking at the top. Instead, leaders simply do what has always been done. While most actions are easy to do and can be completed quickly, corporate strategies are generally multi-year plans that involve repeatedly doing the things listed in Table 1-1 to realize the planned pecuniary gain.

Table 1-1 does not suggest that these actions must never be taken, jointly or severally, nor does it suggest that these are the only options to increase equity market capitalization or enterprise value. Nor does Table 1-1 suggest that all actions listed move a company towards monopoly. Instead, it shows the actions that can be taken singly or in combination to increase pecuniary gain, several of which are used to move a company towards the final goal of monopoly.

An essential observation from Table 1-1 is that corporate strategies are more the same than different. Why is that? Is it because:

- It is the fundamental nature of business?
- Options are limited by business exigencies?
- Economic preconceptions are deeply rooted?

Table 1-1: CEOs Wealth Creation Playbook

Strategies for Pecuniary Gain	Degree of Difficulty (10 = highest)	Time to Execute (years)
Layoffs	1	<1
Hire New Managers	1	<<1
Close Facilities	1	<1
Stock Buy-Backs	1	1-3
Acquisition	2	1-2
Merger	2	1-2
Divestiture / Spinoff	2	1
Change Incentive Compensation	1	<1
Develop New Products	2	1-2
Develop New Markets	3	1-3
Discontinue Products / Services	1	<<1
Reduce / Increase Debt	1	<1
Change Accounting Method	2	1
Incorporate Offshore (inversion)	2	1
Consolidate Operations	2	1-2
Technology / Automation / Digitization	1	1-2
Outsource	2	1-2
Squeeze Suppliers on Prices	1	<1
Price Cuts / Price Increases	1	<<1
Sales Promotions	2	1
Patent Term Extension	2	1-2
Budget Cuts	1	<1
Seek Lower Taxes and Less Regulation	2	1-3

- Copying peers is socially respectful and honorific?
- Maintaining traditions matter more than progress?
- As the company becomes more successful and bureaucratic, problem-solving capabilities deteriorate?
- Top leaders are too busy or burned-out to think?
- Top leaders lack creativity and imagination?
- Top leaders are lazy?
- Top leaders do not think for themselves?
- Top leaders have no desire or incentive to do things differently?

It is, most likely, a combination of all the above (see Note 6). More than being simply explanatory, the above list enumerates several opportunities for productive change and improvement.

Business strategy to increase pecuniary gain can be formal in the sense of a multi-year acquisition and divestiture plan to gain leverage over pricing and other contractual terms, a multi-year plan to produce critical components previously purchased from suppliers to lower costs or control production, or a multi-year plan to control production and distribution. Each of these, in their own way, has some effect to reduce competition that is generally seen as annoying, undesirable, and which generates distasteful and unnecessary work for leaders. These results-oriented leaders are held in much higher esteem by their peers and by society than the leaders who think favorably of competition. They are revered for having tamed the disorderly competitive market, commonly seen as the result of superior intelligence, and for having made themselves wealthy or wealthier.

In addition to formalized business strategy such which has been previously described, there also exists routine standing or evergreen business strategy to increase pecuniary gain. These strategies include:

- Replace labor with technology
- Hold down or reduce workers' wages
- Increase overhead in the forms of executive pay and numbers of managers (see Note 7)
- Raise prices to customers a few times a year or otherwise when circumstances allow it (e.g., shortages, natural or man-made)
- Continuously beat suppliers down on prices
- Neglect investment in research and development
- Starve operations or other departments of resources
- Cull workers from the company when needed

Artificial intelligence algorithms and machine learning are now added to the list of evergreen corporate strategies to increase pecuniary gain. Companies that effectively combine formalized business strategy and evergreen corporate strategies are said to be "well positioned in the marketplace" – meaning, investors can expect above average returns for some time to come. Yet, there will always be a measure of complacency that comes with success and which will one day become apparent.

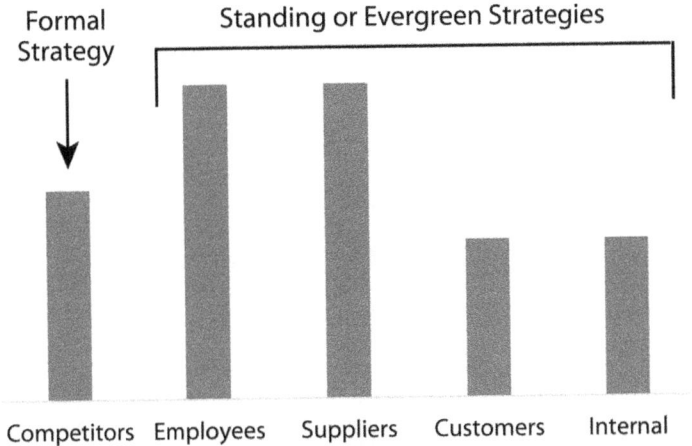

Figure 1-2. Strategy types available to business leaders for gain at the expense of other internal or external stakeholders.

Corporate pecuniary strategy invariably runs along the lines of a plan to save money, make more money, or both. Given the great seriousness of the matter (money-gain), there are important aspects of strategy that go beyond the simple realm of corporate pecuniary gain – ownership of property – into the complex realm of social status, power, political influence, reputability, success, honor, dignity, and personal wealth. This is the subject of Chapter 2.

But before getting to that it must be noted that there is often an unfortunate collision between business strategy to save money, make more money, or both, and the social realm. Being a human construct, it is in the nature of business strategy to have embedded within it faulty assumptions, cognitive biases, and illogical thinking. Rarely are these defects recognized or corrected by strategists *a priori*. But they are usually known by people in the lower ranks, and the defects become splendidly apparent to all when strategies fail. Defects, being intrinsic to all corporate strategies, coupled with leaders' rigid adherence to plans and aversion to bad news, establish the basic conditions for failure. This will be the subject of Chapter 3.

Notes

1. The term "sabotage," as used here, refers to maneuvers made by business leaders that are within the bounds of the law, though perhaps not in its spirit [1]. The purpose of sabotage is to gain pecuniary advantage in relation to one's property and can include withholding something of value from another party or to impede their efficient functioning. Familiar examples of sabotage include withholding or reducing the supply of crude oil, removing airplanes (seat capacity) from air travel, reduce hospital beds through consolidation, information asymmetry (e.g., high-frequency in trading financial securities) – all for the purpose of increasing prices, disadvantaging customers and competitors, or both. Business can sabotage government through tax avoidance which increases government budget deficits or low minimum wage which results in increased spending for government assistance, and, in some cases, they can sabotage government, customers, and competitors, e.g., the sub-prime mortgage financial crisis, where customers enticed to overleverage and governments were forced to bail out insolvent financial institutions who knowingly or unknowingly had the greatest risk exposure.

2. This being a shift from competitive buyers' markets that favors buyers' interests to sellers' markets that favor sellers' interests; a shift from working to get something to getting something for nothing. As the original intent of receiving a corporate charter was to benefit society as a whole, sellers' markets run in the opposite direction of that – though allowable for certain unique purposes such as patents,

trademarks, and copyrights. Yet the more-or-less wholesale transformation of corporate activity from that which benefits society to that which mostly benefits the seller could form a logical basis for dispute.

3. Legally, monopoly is seen as that which causes harm to consumers or other businesses. It is not yet legally seen as resulting in harm to shareholders, non-executive employees, and perhaps others due to management indolence or complacency (and resulting lack of responsiveness and progress). Alternatively, a strategic march towards monopoly could be legally construed as a unique form of self-dealing and insider trading. Often, the turn towards monopoly is accompanied by a turn in executive interest towards substantially increasing financial leverage (borrowed capital) so as to further achieve pecuniary gain. Harvesting the company for leverage puts it at a great disadvantage when competition one day returns (but perhaps little disadvantage in recession because most lenders will be eager to refinance loans at higher rates). Leverage in business is odd in the sense that it is unlike anything an engineer would do. In designing structures such as bridges, engineers employ a safety factor of 2.5 to 3 (material strength divided by design load) to account for unknown factors that may come into play over the lifetime of the structure. Despite minutely characterized material properties, precise calculations, detailed blueprints, exacting methods of construction, and varied types and forms of precise quality inspection, safety factors are needed because of uncertainty and the risk of human injury or death. In corporate finance, the opposite occurs. It is said to be unwise, even foolhardy,

for capital to not be put to work to generate pecuniary gain. The nonproductivity of money is disallowed to the greatest extent possible and employed in search of further opportunities for conquest and exploit. The standing prescription is to "free-up capital" and put it to work. Corporations that are highly leveraged have a "safety factor" of 0.02 to 0.2 (cash divided by debt). Is it possible that business can be more certain than engineering? Does it make sense to "free-up steel" from the bridge design and put it to work in some other structure, thus reducing the safety factor to 1 or less? No, it does not. But such is the odd thinking of business that has long been in play. The consequence of this is difficulty in responding to recessions in an economy that has a 2.5 sigma level of quality (20 percent failure rate). Leveraged businesses are thus drivers, and casualties, of business cycles, pandemics, and other forms of calamity. The received wisdom of monopoly and leverage, handed from one generation of leaders to another, unquestioningly, needs to be reexamined given the risk of harm to humans. Business survival, to the extent that it is desired, is possible when the gospel of leverage is questioned [4].

4. Business success is invariably and uncritically seen as evidence of great intelligence and wisdom. More often it is the result of prowess, cunning, chicanery, and the application of force and fraud; i.e. anticompetitive practice.

5. There is no shortage of books or consulting advice on strategy execution given its high apparent failure rate [5]. This advice can propel a company towards its goal more

quickly and efficiently. The question is, is a moving towards monopoly really where senior leaders want to go? While surely an interesting challenge, the strategy is likely to be more wasteful than it is productive, regardless of its run – a strategy of maladjustment or sabotage.

6. We can further elaborate on the sameness of business strategy by considering leaders' common view of business as a) static (as in maintaining the status quo), b) atomized into its individual (hierarchical, functional, and departmental) components, c) the senior leaders' nonproductive employment (which induces no pressure for imagination), and d) the network of preconceptions [3] that retard the absorption of facts. Learning through ideation requires a different set of understanding: a) evolutionary perspective of continuous change both internally and externally, b) holistic dynamic systems, c) productive work (characterized by sensory perceptions), and d) scientific (critical) thinking to ascertain the facts and discover truth. The second set is knowledge-making practices (KMP) that probe human imagination and creativity, while the first set is knowledge-preserving practices (KPP) that shun originality. Most leaders, having come up through the ranks, start with KMP but quickly transition to KPP when promoted to middle management and higher ranks. The changes in status subjects leaders to the ever-increasing coercive demands of the "institution of leadership" and conformance to its strictures, of which KPP is a central requirement.

7. Executive compensation is essentially a guaranteed expenditure (fixed expense) regardless of business

performance or market conditions. As such, it results in year-over-year increases in overhead costs. Additionally, large companies, especially, suffer from management bloat, which also contributes to high overhead costs. As nonproductive employees, they are a tax on the goods and services sold, much in the same way as advertising and other forms of promotion and conspicuous visibility. Prices must cover these and all other types and quantities of waste engendered by business rivalry and the furtherance of corporate and individual status.

References

[1] Veblen, T. (1904), *The Theory of Business Enterprise*, Charles Scribner's Sons, New York, New York

[2] Thiel, P. (2014), "Competition is for Losers," *The Wall Street Journal*, 12 September, https://www.wsj.com/articles /peter-thiel-competition-is-for-losers-1410535536, accessed 19 December 2020

[3] Emiliani, B. (2018), *The Triumph of Classical Management Over Lean Management: How Tradition Prevails and What to Do About It*, Cubic LLC, South Kingstown, Rhode Island, p. 34

[4] Dooley, B. and Ueno, H. (2020), "This Japanese Shop Is 1,020 Years Old. It Knows a Bit About Surviving Crises," *The New York Times*, Section B, Page 1, 2 December, https://nyti.ms/2VxeMkR, accessed 29 December 2020

[4] Cândido, C. and Santos, S. (2015), "Strategy Implementation: What is the Failure Rate?" *Journal of Management & Organization*, Vol. 21, No. 2, 237-262. http://dx.doi.org/10.1017/jmo.2014.77

2

Social Science
of Strategy

Social Science of Strategy

Business leaders engage in activities that are commensurate with their high status and which brings them honor. Historically, the employments that brought highest honors were those involved with exploit in some form or another. These included warfare, sports, government, and priestly service [1]. Business leadership is close in form to each of these types of employment. Warfare in the sense of war-like strategies of conquest. Sport in the sense of hunting, gamesmanship, and negotiation. Government in the sense of leaders ruling over the masses, making policy, and meting punishment and reward. Priestly service in the sense of fortune telling (predicting the future; e.g. "forward-looking statements"), presiding over sacred and ceremonial forms of information sharing (executive retreats, shareholder meetings, all-employee meetings), and superintendence of venerated objects (policies, strategic plans, financial statements, patents, trademarks).

These employments are of a distinctly different class and character than the people employed to perform labor; the work of producing goods and services at the frontline and others who are adjacent to it. These people, the workers, the doers, toil in industrious work for their sustenance whereas business leaders are exempt from menial labor and associated drudgery. The business leader's activities – warfare, sports, government, and priestly service – are non-industrious and thus nonproductive. The division of labor is a differentiation in function and therefore a differentiation in class upon which distinction is, by nature, invidious.

Strategy demands shrewdness, cunning, and prowess, which is recognized as separate and of a higher order than the knowledge and skills that one must possess to do productive industrious work. It requires freedom from empathy, honesty, misgiving, human welfare, and worry. It is a nonimaginative and noncreative occupation. Those skilled in industrious work have no sanction or ability to formulate business strategy. Their impractical business mind, formed by the productive workaday habits of process, procedure, logic, cause and effect, diligence, goodwill, and concern for others make them unfit to traffic in exploit or even to advise upon the matter. Those lower down the hierarchy, whose employment is by the grace of their leader, expect the top leader to formulate effective strategy even though their understanding of it or its consequences is usually paper thin.

Strategy, in its march toward monopoly, involves deal-making. It is a purposeful plan of aggression, of exploit, to seize something of value; to gain "something" for doing "nothing" that is productive. Strategy is, in some way or another, a plan to injure or destroy things – jobs, product lines, facilities, customers, competitors, and communities – collateral damage in pursuit of pecuniary gain, legitimized by varied economic and business preconceptions and rationalized by society as "creative destruction" that is both necessary and useful. The strategists' plans are commensurate with their fundamental employments – warfare, sport, government, and priestly service.

Negotiation and deal-making confer glory, social status,

reputability, and honor. It earns the esteem of others. The lesser work of strategy execution, is, where possible, delegated to others. Their task is to attend to the drudgery of details, to get their hands dirty and execute their leader's or their client's plan. The leader's employment is to think while others do. Any difficulties they encounter are not the leader's problem for the strategy is always sound by virtue of its source. Such glory cannot be had by only one, it must be had by all who are highest in rank. The appetite for exploit and seizure becomes sharpened by invidious comparison and results in widespread emulation. The motive force of emulation and peer pressure to perform, to do as one's peers do, requires others to play for better position in the marketplace. It is a struggle between leaders over the ownership of private property, and such struggles are honorific because they offer the sizeable reward of proving one's prowess and worth. Those who do not undertake such feats of exploit, who have no strategic plan or who inherit strategic plans from their predecessors, are judged to be lesser leaders.

People occupying positions wherein their employ is nonproductive must, necessarily, find something to do that is, or appears to be, useful. The higher one's position, the more it is required to do things that are commensurate with one's status and scrupulously avoid anything that could result in the appearance of weakness or the debasement of one's honor, dignity, character, or importance. The requirement is to show superior strength, status, and intelligence, and collect trophies that symbolize shrewdness, cunning, and prowess. In business, the method that produces the highest accolades is to purposefully alter the field of natural competition [2] – to transform the environment – for the teleological end of pecuniary gain. Businesses best adapted to their environment, whether customer base or location (e.g., local businesses) cannot, in the end, be permitted to survive. They must be overtaken for pecuniary gain, while said to be in the name of eliminating waste and inefficiency. The larger forms of business crowd out the smaller forms [3, 4], fit as the latter may be in their own environment. The tangible benefit is to self and imagined to society (see Chapter 1, Note 4).

The practical art and science of overcoming vexatious competition – designing, calculating, prognosticating – is a unique field of knowledge whose product is the strategic plan. The plan is an owned property that is gratifying in and of itself. It is a source of esteem and a basis for invidious comparison as the plan slowly unfolds in the daylight of business and delivers the expected laurels within one's industry or among all CEOs. It establishes a personal rating, usually in money-terms (value of the deal or stock price), to compare worth and repute. To not have a business strategy would be an unwelcome departure from the required standards of decorum, status, and honor resulting in disapproval among one's peers. Top leaders must have strategies (Figure 2-1).

Business strategy is widely recognized as having value for other reasons such as upholding ancient traditions and accredited habits of thought. In this sense, strategy is of a ceremonial nature and it includes performing the many related social and festive duties as required by one's status.

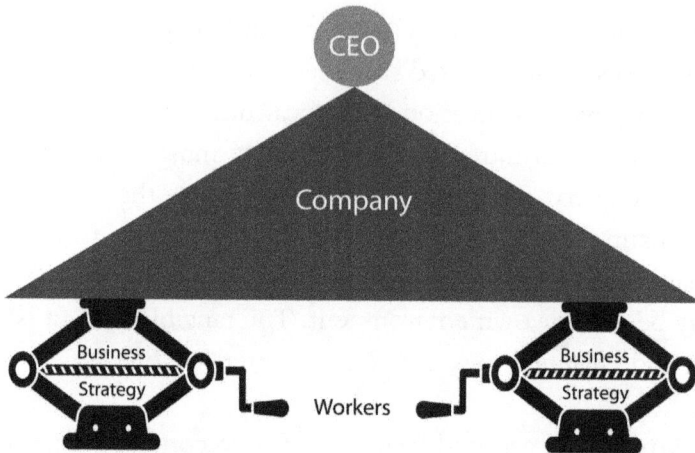

Figure 2-1. The aim of business strategy is to lift the leader and the company to greater heights of pecuniary gain.

It fulfills both spiritual [5] and practical business requirements. Thus, business must be conducted in requisite form to assure that one's service is meritorious. Business strategy is also of value as a consequence of its inverse; its absence exposes one to the stain of unworthiness as a business leader.

Given its great practical and spiritual value, the construction of strategy spares no expense. Costly executive time is taken up in strategy development such that whatever is produced must, by its existence, be needed, intellectually rigorous, and accurate. Strategy is reputable to a higher grade and aesthetically more pleasing when it is grandiose in scale and scope and expensive to create and execute. Thriftiness is vulgar. Executive time is further taken up by the periodic review of progress made in strategy execution by the assigned teams whose status and honor come by way of reflection from and close proximity to the strategist. The lower levels know, or quickly learn, that it is impolite and indecorous to question the strategists' strategy.

The preoccupation with business strategy is permitted under the generally false assumption that all is going well in the day-to-day operation of the business (see Note 1), and that there is no need for leaders to understand low-level problems or lend a helping hand so that one's hirelings can succeed. These interfere with the quest for pecuniary gain. Such assistance to the lower levels is regarded as inglorious and dishonorable and thus, by right, to be avoided. Though, from paying customers' perspective, one's usefulness is inversely proportional to their status in the hierarchy.

How deviant it is that esteemed business leaders commonly claim a great love for business – ostensibly for the learning, problem-solving, interaction with people, and customer satisfaction – while simultaneously inflicting injury and destruction through business strategy bent on pecuniary gain (see Note 2). This incongruity assures that business remains in a perpetual state of chaos, presenting a flood of opportunity for further exploit, injury, and destruction to ferociously parade one's love of business. It is a playground for the uninhibited mind.

Business leaders are driven for "more" of specific types: more sales, more growth, more profit, more market share, more employees, more products and services, and so on (see Notes 3 and 4). Good numbers can fool leaders into thinking progress has been made. War-like business strategy is a strategy for more, an empire-building strategy and rulership over a vast dominion of enterprises with an eye towards a quasi-dynastic succession. The vision, whether it is a private dream with no chance of being realized or tangible action converted to reality, is grandiose. It can be that for some time, but it is not ever-lasting due to defects intrinsic to the strategy and the multitude of errors made subsequently by people in all levels of the organization, every day. The quest for dominance and maintenance of dominance generates thousands of large and small mistakes over time. The strategy is destined to fail, and so it is only a question of when.

The above discussion makes obvious the connection between the social science of strategy and the proliferation of mistakes and errors that will occur. Much of this is driven by struggles between the top and the bottom of the corporate hierarchy to ascertain the truth of the situation. The former, being far more likely to prevail, crowds out (suffocates) the latter. It often comes down to "I am superior in rank. Therefore, I know better than you." Furthermore, it is apparent that social constraints and obligations and business conservatism are principal causes of the lack of creativity found in business strategy.

• • • •

Strategy is a human construct, one that does not exist in the same form or purpose in Nature. In business, strategy is conceived in impersonal calculating ways and deployed to achieve a desired teleological end more quickly – "owning the market." In Nature, proliferation of a single species would crowd out other species and be detrimental to the local environment. Instead, a vibrant ecological environment has abundant variety produced by the ability of flora and fauna to generate many potential offspring. Maple trees release hundreds of thousands of seeds (samaras, colloquially referred to as "helicopters") to produce a few hundred saplings. Dandelion flowers and tomatoes produce 150 to 300 seeds in hope that a dozen seeds will germinate to perpetuate the species. Some species of fish spawn tens of thousands of eggs to assure the survival of a few. Nature sees it as wisest to do the opposite of what business leaders do – multiply the chances for success rather than reduce them.

The same could be done in business, to allow a more natural commercial environment to exist and thrive. Instead of crowding out competitors such that the environment consists of only a few species of large business to serve market needs, the leaders of large corporations could produce as many offspring as possible – start-up companies with backing from the parent and a readymade base of customers. It has the resources to do this productive work, just as it has the resources to do the opposite. And they could help repopulate the small business ecosystem after economic disasters such as recessions and COVID-19. Some start-ups will survive as they grow and adapt to changing circumstances, and they will, in turn, spawn more small start-up companies. This natural unfolding of local competition will give the weak opportunities to survive and the more robust to prosper. The parent organization can remain a minority or majority owner and the offspring would pay dividends or a share of profits to its parent. These relationships can be developed to serve local customer's ever-changing interests such as sharing of resources and know-how.

Strategy necessarily entails a gamble in relation to its development, due to preconceptions and cognitive biases, and execution – e.g., the expected outcomes such as synergies and increases in stock price. Often, combinations of businesses fail to realize synergies and are net destroyers of shareholder value due to increased bureaucracy and conservatism among leaders who become more focused on retaining dominance than understanding and providing what customers want. Gambling is always a lowering of one's intelligence because of its animistic roots. Economic efficiency in the material world lies in facts and causal sequence, not in gambling and luck to deliver the desired wins. Supernatural explanations of phenomena result in a continuous build-up of ignorance of cause and effect based on sensory perceptions. Senior leaders must increase their intelligence, but they can do that only by emancipating themselves from their peers whose embrace of the status quo and unrelenting obedience to outdated preconceptions and the demand for war-like business strategies of "more" (Figure 2-2).

Business leaders can instead learn from Nature and raise their intelligence. They can think how Nature solves

Economic

Spiritual

Social

Social
Science
of
Strategy

Business

Political

Legal

Historical

Philosophical

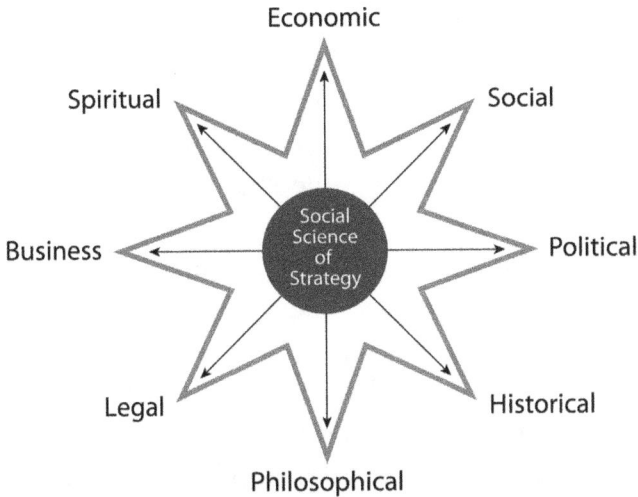

Figure 2-2. Business strategy bent on pecuniary gain is informed by a network of interrelated preconceptions. Each category contains ten to fifteen preconceptions.

problems; how it maintains healthy and balanced local environments [6], and how Nature adapts to changing circumstances. Adaptation is as more of a sure thing and adaptation raises intelligence. Yet leaders' need for social status, power, prestige, and honor are non-negotiable requirements. These come easily via the time-worn route as previously described, the march toward monopoly, at least until the sentiments of society or politicians change. The social standing and accolades that leaders require can be easily gained by doing the opposite; by launching many offspring. It is a choice between socially productive work and nonproductive parasitic work.

Some metrics for success will remain the same and some will change. More sales, more growth, more profit, more market share, more employees, and more products and services give way to number of offspring, total sales generated by offspring, number of public and private offspring, total wealth created by offspring, number employed by offspring, and the like. The honor will be in parentage, jobs, development, and evolution, not ownership, size, and scale. Wealth is sure to be created by this new method as was under the old scheme, both personal and business. It simply a matter of using one's intelligence to figure out how to do it, but in ways that do not rely on exploit, injury, or destruction (see Note 5). Make it a jobs-based business ecosystem rather than shareholder-based busines ecosystem [7], one that provides both living wages and adequate returns to shareholders (see Note 6). It is an evolution from ignoble leadership that murders the human spirit to a noble leadership that respects humanity, especially the workers who are the living medium through which business success is achieved.

Business leaders, conservative as most are, will vigorously defend the status quo against this form of disruption and the unraveling of beloved preconceptions, learning, and methods of warfare, sports, government, and priestly service. They will be skeptical and defensive of any alteration to the pragmatism of exploit, seizure, cunning, and prowess as it has been understood for centuries. They will surely consider this change to be a total surrender of the beneficent system of pecuniary gain that ably served them and their forebears. Change can be a trifling affair for some or a trauma for others. Those leading change will at first be marginalized as outliers, while those in arrears will, over time, face a decline in esteem driven by a growing intolerance for exploit, injury, and destruction.

This chapter outlined, in resplendent terms, lesser-known features and facts of the social science of strategy. It illuminates the pitfalls of business strategy and an alternative better aligned with Nature. Given that the former is likely to prevail for the calculable future, one can predict the high likelihood of numerous consequential errors in strategy development and execution. That is the subject of Chapter 3.

If, as a senior leader and strategist, you have been able to make it to this point in the book, your reward follows.

Notes

1. It is a false assumption because leaders are typically told what they want to hear, and performance metrics are often gamed to produce the desired result. These two abnormalities, combined with other irregularities, produce a false or overly optimistic representation of actual conditions.

2. The more typical reasons why leaders love business is self-regarding: being the boss, telling people what to do, higher remuneration, winning, honor, respect, admiration, etc. The love for business centers mostly on being the recipient of mass affection. Leaders' fondness for monopoly and other anticompetitive practices takes them to as close as one can to being a king or queen, allowing them to reap the bounty of compulsory affection that attends the second highest level of status.

3. In recent decades, the path to becoming a CEO has been increasingly through the position as CFO (where this is not the case, the CFO usually has an outsized influence on the CEO). Training in accountancy coupled with a strategy of pecuniary gain can result in exploit internally, within the organization, as well as externally among stakeholders. The internal exploit is particularly interesting as its focus is invariably to save money for the purpose of increasing profits. This starves internal functions of resources need to do good work and typically manifests itself in varied problems stemming from poor quality or deficiency in one or another form of internal control (such as information

system security). The accountant who faithfully views the spreadsheet and budgets as more highly accredited versions of reality than reality itself is doomed to fuck-up. It is only a question of when and by how much.

4. The quest for more includes, at times, an almost pathological need by leaders to acquire businesses and product lines. Serially collecting properties resembles a type of hoarding behavior whose intent is to gain control, reduce threats, or achieve a form of perfection in one's duties. In most cases, leaders overpay for acquisitions which typically leads to injury and destruction of the acquired property in search of pecuniary gain. Serially collecting properties generates corporate clutter that becomes increasingly difficult to effectively lead and manage. Intelligent people high in status believe they have a preternatural (or perhaps supernatural) ability to handle complexity. Despite a heroic self-image, corporate clutter usually results in the impairment of leaders' duties; impairment that they are likely unaware and others reluctant to inform. The wise simplify that which is complex, the unwise seek that which is simplistic.

5. While businesses are owned by shareholders, it is also true that without customers the shareholders would own next to nothing. So, in a sense, customers are owners too, and as such they should be rewarded with their own benefit of lower prices when the company achieves cost savings through process improvement or other non-destructive means (e.g., reduction in fixed and variable expenses such as office space, advertising, etc.). This "customer dividend"

would be a feature of businesses that are more concordant with Nature – cooperation, mutual benefit, and improvement instead of exploit, injury, and destruction.

6. When we think of returns to shareholders, we commonly think in the range of seven to 15 percent. Yet in this age of near zero interest rates, investors have shown themselves to be satisfied with rates of return of one to four percent. A jobs-based business ecosystem would likely produce returns in that range, and possibly a bit higher. Thus, investors could be sufficiently satisfied in ways other than the traditional shareholder-based busines ecosystem.

References

[1] Veblen, T. (1899), *The Theory of the Leisure Class: An Economic Study of Institutions*, Macmillan Co., New York, New York

[2] Ward, L.F. (1893), "The Psychologic Basis of Social Economics," *The Annals of the American Academy of Political and Social Science*, January, Volume 3, pp. 72-90, https://www.jstor.org/stable/1008913

[3] Marrioli, D. (2020), "How Amazon Wins: By Steamrolling Rivals and Partners," *The Wall Street Journal*, 22 December, https://www.wsj.com/articles/amazon-competition-shopify-wayfair-allbirds-antitrust-11608235127, accesses 22 December 2020

[4] Mitchell, S. (2006), *Big-Box Swindle: The True Cost of Mega-Retailers and the Fight for America's Independent Businesses*, Beacon Press, Boston, Massachusetts

[5] Emiliani, B. (2020), *Management Mysterium: The Quest for Progress*, Cubic LLC, South Kingstown, Rhode Island

[6] See the Institute for Local Self-Reliance, https://ilsr.org, accessed 26 December 2020

[7] Goodman, P. (2020), "Co-ops in Spain's Basque Region Soften Capitalism's Rough Edges," *The New York Times*, 29 December, https://nyti.ms/34QxadR, accessed 30 December 2020

3
Strategy Failure
Analysis

Strategy Failure Analysis

The success orientation of business leaders means that they will claim credit for successes and quickly distance themselves from failure. This behavior is an obvious manifestation of status and wealth and a desire to preserve honor, reputation, and worth. But it also reveals an attitude of infallibility or immunity from mistakes and thus an unwillingness to learn from one's own mistakes. It further suggests an unwillingness to learn from mistakes made by other business leaders, particularly when they occur in industries that are different from their own.

Blame and scapegoating are ubiquitous when failure occurs (see Note 1). Sometimes leaders will support an internal investigation of the failure, more usually others lower in the hierarchy are assigned the task of learning from the mistakes. Whether *ad hoc* or structured, the lessons learned from failure rarely has any impact in an organization. Either the analysis of the failure did not reveal the root causes or the findings were ignored under the assumption that the same mistakes are unlikely to happen again. Superficiality is characteristic of such efforts because the truth, generally unbearable, is even less bearable under such difficult circumstances. Also lacking is curiosity to know what really happened and trust in self and others that enables reflection.

Strategy development and execution, like other decision-making processes, contain myriad opportunities for mistakes. Some are easy to detect in real-time, others become apparent after the failure occurs. Mistakes detected in real-time often go uncorrected because of a goal, timeline, or other restriction mandated by senior leaders that prevents the truth (facts) from coming out and making needed corrections. Expediency interferes with strategy development and execution, as does the status quo. Mistakes that are apparent subsequent to the failure are, most often, soon forgotten as the exigencies of business demand that people focus their attention elsewhere.

Usually, the most superficial and least accurate causal explanations for failure are proffered by senior leaders, often externalized to the weather, competitors, shifts in the marketplace, or other factors not easily disproven by outsiders. These explanations rarely go challenged and thus prevail, allowing people to return to their regular duties as if nothing happened. Senior leaders, being concerned about appearance, "optics," and, ultimately, aesthetics in relation to themselves and the business [1] are quick to expel failure and cleanse themselves and the business. Yet, the same mistakes that led to failure are likely to be repeated and result in similar failures in the future, whether under the same or new leadership. Leaders use the same wealth creation playbook, over and over again (see Chapter 1, Table 1-1), thus increasing the likelihood of repeat failures of the same or similar types.

Almost always missing from business failure analysis is a structured method or process for analyzing failures. There is no method unique to the business world, perhaps because its success orientation and avoidance of responsibility preclude construction of a specialized method of analysis.

When failure analysis methods are used, they are usually taken from the technical domain of engineering failures. These methods can be very helpful at identifying higher order technical causes, but they may de-emphasize or leave out the human factors that subtend decision-making – the shared preconceptions, cognitive biases, assumptions, and illogical thinking that define business and how leaders think.

While the consequence of business strategy failure can be deadly to individuals and corporations and cause serious injuries to stakeholders, formal methods of failure analysis are not taught in business school. Nor are they part of executive development training programs. Formal failure analysis would be a more productive route to improving executive skills given that both higher education and corporate leadership development programs are usually disconnected from real-world context and the serious consequences resulting from defective leadership thinking and decision-making. Their dreamy focus on the glorious aspects of business and leadership necessarily comes at the expense of intellectual rigor and thus meaningful improvements to corporate governance.

Overview of Strategy Failure Analysis Method

What follows is an example of the four-part Strategy Failure Analysis Method (SFAM) developed by the first author (Emiliani, see Note 2). We analyze Boeing's sales and growth strategy as it relates to the 737 Max commercial airplane. This case consists of both technical design and engineering failures (upgrading an old aircraft design one too many times, forward engine configuration, single angle of attack sensor, and the maneuvering characteristics augmentation system (MCAS), and strategy failures pertaining to both saving money and making more money (sales, profits, growth). Our focus will be Boeing leaderships' strategy to save money and make more money – not the technical engineering failure – but their strategy of conquest over rival Airbus and of exploit for pecuniary gain.

Teaching strategy failure analysis begins by asking managers the answers that wish to obtain from learning the method. They want to:

- Learn how and why leaders arrive at their decisions.
- Understand why leaders disregard others safety when making decisions.
- Learn why leaders disregard facts especially when the facts prevent harm to people.
- Know why leaders have a hard time admitting mistakes or failures.
- Learn how leaders can avoid making bad decisions.
- Learn how to prevent future problems from repeating.

Next, they are challenged to identify questions they must ask to ascertain the answers listed above. These include:

- What sequence of steps are taken to make decisions?
- How often are negative effects considered in decision-making?

- Why don't leaders feel obligated to think of the greater good?
- How often does money influence decision-making?
- Why do leaders minimize or ignore unfavorable consequences?
- What causes leaders to simply ignore the facts?
- How much personal belief and ego is involved in ignoring facts?
- Why do leaders think they know better than the facts?
- How are bad decisions linked to corporate culture, customer, or societal expectations?
- Why do leaders let reputation get in the way of admitting failure?
- How can leaders overcome fear of admitting mistakes and failures?
- How can leaders learn to think more logically at all times?
- What are the traps that lead to bad decisions?
- How should leaders rely on workers to improve decision-making?

The start of the failure analysis process has managers think in ways that they have probably thought little about before. Leaders' success orientation diminishes thought of failure, the causes of failure, and its varied consequences. As a leader, do you think about these 14 questions regularly? If not, why not? These are wonderful questions to reflect upon. Refer to Chapters 1 and 2 for some answers.

The failure analysis requires a careful reading of articles detailing the failure from various sources, arranged chronologically (see Note 3). The reading pack can be as little as 50 pages or as much as 750 pages (see Note 4). Generally, the reading pack is 200-300 pages. It requires some work to read and re-read the articles to digest the information and then produce the four-part failure analysis. Some iterative revision to each of the four parts is necessary to produce a good quality failure analysis and to incorporate serviceable learning into leadership practice.

Part One of the failure analysis begins by identifying the stakeholders that senior leaders were most concerned about prior to the failure followed by identifying which stakeholders senior leaders were most concerned about after to the failure. The stakeholders are customers, employees, suppliers, investors, competitors, community, government, and themselves (i.e., company or leaders). Stakeholders and leaders' concerns about them usually differ after the failure compared to before the failure. This indicates a significant shift in senior management concern that was either not present or ill-considered when the strategy was developed. The next steps are to summarize the current state after the failure occurred, identify what senior leaders did to address the problem, identify inconsistencies between what senior leaders said and what they did, and identify beliefs and untested assumptions the senior leaders had that contributed to the problem. The "say-do" inconsistencies reveal shifting or capricious leadership, while the beliefs and untested assumptions establish a foundation upon which the failure usually rests.

Part Two of the failure analysis begins by identifying the "effect" – the big bad thing that happened. The effect is used as the basis for determining both traditional and process-based causal relationships. This leads to an identification of the biggest, but by no means sole, driver of the failure. Part Three is a formal root cause analysis, starting with the "effect" previously identified, followed by the identification of practical countermeasures. This is generally where people stumble. They believe themselves to be good at analyzing cause and effect, but are actually very poor at it, and the countermeasures they identify are either ineffective or impractical. For most people, Part Three requires a few rounds of revision to identify the actual cause and the countermeasures that are indeed practical and which can be implemented.

Part Four begins by identifying the existence of cognitive biases (a reality created by one's biases) possessed by senior leaders that were operative in the failure. While there are nearly 200 types of cognitive biases, the failure analysis process asks to focus on the half-dozen or so those that are most common. The subsequent step is to identify the forms of illogical thinking that were operative in the failure. While there are over 100 forms of illogical thinking, the failure analysis process focuses on the dozen or so major forms. For both cognitive biases and the major forms of illogical thinking, one must identify specific examples from the reading. Examples of illogical thinking are more difficult to identify than examples of cognitive biases. The last element of part four is to identify the significant learnings. These should then be incorporated into a new or existing standard practice used for strategy development and execution.

Boeing's strategy with respect to the 737 Max was a sales and growth strategy; specifically, to save money and make more money. That is a common business strategy, whether it applies to the business as a whole or a specific product line, and thus a recurring theme in failure analysis. The conquest and exploit required to save money or make more money invariably results in penny-wise, pound-foolish decisions – decisions that seem good and right at the time end up being significant causes that produce the unwanted effect, failure.

The leadership decision-making that surrounds strategy development and execution are bounded by certain parameters that are inviolate. In Boeing's case, senior leaders, in concert with the board of directors, wanted to (in random order):

- Reduce the cost of new products
- Reduce the product development timeline
- Modify or upgrade existing products
- Obtain certification more quickly
- Expand the fleet of 737 aircraft
- Reduce pilot training costs to airline customers

This strategy appears to be sound at the executive level. But at the working level – the people who know the most about the product and related development and production processes – problems with each item were apparent from the start. As is often the case, the large gap between the leaders' strategy and the many things that must be done by workers to achieve the strategy go largely unresolved. That is because of the success orientation of leaders, or, conversely, the ludicrous and unrealistic impossibility of failure. Leaders who are disinterested to understand the details of how to make something happen, a phenomenon driven by status (Chapter 2), leads to cost, quality, and delivery problems in product development, problems with the product when it used by customers, or both. It is not their intent for this to happen, but too often that is the outcome – and responsibility for which most leaders work tirelessly to obfuscate and evade.

Strategy Failure Analysis Method – Part One

We begin the analysis of Boeing's 737 Max strategy failure by reviewing selected sections from Part One. Before the Lion Air and Ethiopian Airlines 737 Max crashes that killed 346 people, Boeing senior leaders had the following concerns about stakeholders:

- Customers – Lower cost aircraft operation
- Suppliers – Late deliveries
- Investors – Stock price
- Competitors – Airbus A320 product
- Government – Ease of FAA approvals
- Themselves – Pecuniary gain

After the two deadly airplane crashes, Boeing senior leaders had the following concerns about stakeholders:

- Customers – Convince airlines 737 Max is safe
- Employees – Quick fix to MCAS software
- Investors – Damage control to prop up stock price
- Community – Safety of 737 Max
- Government – FAA investigations
- Themselves – Public image

Post-disasters, there is a shift in stakeholders and senior management's concerns for each stakeholder. Suppliers and Competitors are no longer a concern, Employees and Community become a concern, and the substance of concern about Customers, Government, and Themselves changes. Concern about Investors remains about the same.

Next, what were some of the inconsistencies between what senior leaders said and what the actually did:

- Boeing shifted blame to Lion Air (poor maintenance) and Ethiopian Airlines (pilot errors)
- Boeing said that the MCAS software made the airplane like previous models allowing carriers to upgrade with minimal training cost
- Boeing stated there was no issue – MCAS system was cancelled in the same way as before, but later forced to release advisory and software update
- Boeing and FAA agreed that there was no major requalification required, though clearly there was
- Boeing claims to work closely with test pilots and airline pilots when designing features, yet MCAS modifications were made based on internal

discussion among engineers
- Boeing claims safety is a core value

Some of these inconsistencies would be apparent internally by workers prior to the 737 Max crashes, while others become apparent after the crashes.

Next, what are some of the beliefs and untested assumptions that senior leaders had that contributed to the failure.

- Boeing thought that vintage (50-year-old) 737 design could accommodate bigger engines
- Boeing thought that modernizing vintage 737 would be cheaper than designing a new aircraft to meet airline customer needs
- MCAS produced the same aircraft functionality as earlier versions of 737
- Boeing believed it could convinced airlines and regulators that no additional pilot training was required
- Boeing thought it was acceptable to have single-reliant system vs. redundant system as is the norm in commercial aircraft design
- Boeing engineers calculated probability of catastrophic MCAS malfunction to be virtually impossible
- Boeing said pilots would understand how to override MCAS based on existing checklists and in the 3-second window to take action

Here we can see how beliefs and untested assumptions, which are connected to a status-oriented predisposition to ignore facts and warnings brought by lower-level workers, lays the foundation for the Lion Air and Ethiopian Airlines crashes.

Strategy Failure Analysis Method – Part Two

The next step is to identify causal relationships. The effect, the big bad thing that happened, was 346 people died in two 737 Max aircraft crashes. What caused it? A traditional fishbone diagram has six causal categories: Human, Machine, Methods, Materials, Measures, and Environment. While causalities were assigned to each category, the principal cause categories contributing to the strategy failure were Methods, Measures, and Human. For Methods we find:

- Process for deciding to modernize the 737 (vs. new aircraft design)
- Process for deciding content of pilot's manual
- Process for software review
- Process for aircraft certification
- Process for pilots to diagnose and overcome malfunctions in-flight
- Process for training pilots

For Measures we find:

- 737 Max aircraft sales

- 737 Max profits
- 737 Max deliveries
- Risk assessment (failure probability)
- "Minimal changes" so no new pilot training
- Angle-of-attack, airspeed, altitude data

For Human we find:

- Lack of communication with pilots
- Inter-departmental communication is ineffective
- Casual attitude toward safety
- Withholding information to gain certification
- Pilots not trained to deal with faulty MCAS

Next, we go a step further and identify causality in relation to six business processes: Human Resource Processes, Engineering and New Product Development Processes, Finance Processes, Sales and Marketing Processes, Operations and Supply Processes, and Information or Information Technology Processes. In this case, the principal cause categories contributing to the strategy failure were Engineering and New Product Development Processes, Finance Processes, Sales and Marketing Processes, and Information or Information Technology Processes.

For Engineering and New Product Development Processes we find:

- Reuse 737 design to avoid recertification and pilot training
- MCAS used to offset different flight characteristics to eliminate expensive pilot training
- Single point failure determined to be non-catastrophic because pilots can intervene
- Confusing alarms and displays in flight emergency

For Finance Processes we find:

- Process for deciding to modernize the 737 (vs. new aircraft design)
- Sell as many 737 Max as possible based on similarity to previous models
- Improve profit margin

For Sales and Marketing Processes we find:

- Upgrade of 737, no flight simulator training
- Safety is our primary concern
- We're Boeing. Trust us.

For Information or Information Technology Processes we find:

- Poor information flow within Boeing
- Withheld information from FAA
- Information not passed along to pilots and carriers
- Misunderstood severity of single point of failure

Of the six traditional causal categories and six process causal categories, the single biggest driver of the failure was judged to be Finance Processes. This, of course, connects to the Measures category.

Strategy Failure Analysis Method – Part Three

The next step is to perform a formal root cause analysis using the "5 Whys" method. The root cause analysis is based on the single biggest driver, Finance Processes. Additional root cause analysis can be performed for other of the identified major cause categories – Methods, Human, Engineering and New Product Development Processes, Sales and Marketing Processes, and Information or Information Technology Processes. Here we will focus on the cause category Finance Processes. The 5 Whys analysis is as follows:

1. Why did 346 people die in two 737 Max aircraft crashes?
   – MCAS forced the plane into a nosedive.
2. Why did MCAS force the plane into a nosedive?
   – MCAS was responding to a single faulty angle of attack sensor showing a dangerous stall condition.
3. Why was MCAS responding to a single faulty sensor?
   – MCAS was designed to use inputs from only one flight computer's data stream.
4. Why was MCAS only designed to use only one flight computer's data stream?
   – Engineers deemed a single point of failure to be non-catastrophic.

5. Why did engineers deem single point of failure to be non-catastrophic?
   - Pilots could intervene using the same procedure for previous 737 models.
6. Why could the pilots intervene using the same procedure for previous 737 models?
   - MCAS software was created to provide similar flight handling characteristics.
7. Why was MCAS software created to provide similar flight characteristics?
   - To get carriers to upgrade their existing fleet of 737s
8. Why did Boeing want carriers to upgrade their existing fleet of 737s?
   - To sell more airplanes.
9. Why did Boeing want to sell more planes?
   - Generate higher revenues and profits.
10. Why did Boeing want to generate higher revenues and profits?
   - To make the company more valuable; specifically, higher stock price.

This root cause is consistent with other findings in relation to Boeing's senior leadership's strategy and decision-making with respect to the 737 Max.

What practical countermeasure can be applied to prevent such a failure from happening again? Note that this is a repeat failure for Boeing, having encountered numerous problems in strategy (save money) and execution of the 787 commercial aircraft program, wherein lower-level people's warnings were also ignored [2, 3].

At the fourth why, "Why was MCAS only designed to use only one flight computer's data stream?", a practical countermeasure would be:

- Return to the practice of redundant systems to help prevent catastrophic events.

At the seventh why, "Why was MCAS software created to provide similar flight characteristics?", a practical countermeasure would be:

- Upgrades and "like platforms" should have more oversight rather than relying on manufacturer to determine similarity.

At the eighth why, "Why did Boeing want carriers to upgrade their existing fleet of 737s?", a practical countermeasure would be:

- Focus on customers' needs, not the company's needs.

At the tenth why, "Why did Boeing want to generate higher revenues and profits?", a practical countermeasure would be:

- Change senior leaders' incentives and compensation to focus on customer-centered rather than company-centered performance metrics.

Of course, other countermeasures can be envisioned and implemented. In a complex case such as this, practical countermeasures would have to be identified and implemented at various levels of the causal sequence and evaluated for their effectiveness to avoid repeating this or similar catastrophic failures.

Strategy Failure Analysis Method – Part Four

The next step is to identify the cognitive biases that were operative in the failure and cite specific examples. They are:

- Anchoring (giving disproportionate weight to the first information received)
  - ▶ MCAS could never cause a crash; pilots can intervene.

- Status Quo (preference for solutions that preserve the current state)
  - ▶ Poor maintenance and pilot error are the cause of all accidents.

- Sunk Cost (make decisions that support past decisions)
  - ▶ Reusing 737 platform reduces initial investment cost and drives increased sales.

- Confirming Evidence (seek information that supports your view)
  - ▶ Blame maintenance procedure and pilot error.

- Framing (making decisions based on how a question or problem is framed)
  - ▶ No need to update manuals or training since flight characteristics are the same.

- Estimating and Forecasting (making estimates or forecasts for uncertain events)
  - ▶ Vanishing low probability that MCAS could cause pilot to lose control and cause a crash. Reliance on pilots to function flawlessly under extreme stress events. Boeing slogan: "Safety First."

Here we can see that seasoned executives with decades of experience make fundamental mistakes – systematic errors in thinking – whose consequences were tragic. Senior leaders must always keep in mind how both strategy and execution can be weakened or destroyed by cognitive biases. But it does not end there. All human thinking, particularly in hierarchies where critical thinking is highly discouraged, is subject to various forms of illogic.

The next step is to identify the forms of illogical thinking that were operative in the failure and cite specific examples. They are:

- Denying the Antecedent (if A then B; not A therefore, not B)
  - ▶ If a pilot can override a single point of failure, then the failure cannot be catastrophic.

- Affirming the Consequent (if A then B; B therefore, A)
    - ▶ If new model is the same as the old model, then the new model operates the same as old model.

- False Assumptions (knowing or suspecting the assumption is false but using it anyway)

    - ▶ Maintenance and pilot error. MCAS can't cause an accident. Pilots can correct.

- Using and Abusing Tradition (using tradition to argue against something)
    - ▶ 737 Max engineered to function like earlier models. New aircraft model is too expensive.

- Ad hominem (attack the person, not the argument)
    - ▶ Maintenance technicians and pilots are at fault.

- Avoiding the Force of Reason (make false claims or use power to avoid an argument)
    - ▶ Boeing and FAA forced to ground 737 Max *after* commercial airlines ground the planes.

- Abuse of Expertise (using expertise or experts to justify an action)
    - ▶ MCAS software fixes nose-up problem; design approved with single point of failure.

- Red Herring (divert someone's attention from the problem at hand)
    - ▶ Blame the pilots and mechanics.

- Inability to Disprove Does not Prove (no proof against x does not make a favorable argument for x)
  - ▶ Inability to disprove pilot error does not prove Boeing is not at fault.

- False Dilemma (saying there are only two choices when there are many)
  - ▶ Automated flight control system or manual intervention will avert catastrophe.

- Special Pleading (omitting key information because it would undermine one's position).
  - ▶ Boeing omitted pulling back on the yoke would cancel or that MCAS was different.

- Expediency (ignoring the means to achieve a desired end)
  - ▶ Get the planes acting the same and sell same-as for more profit and to beat Airbus.

Again, we see that seasoned executives with decades of experience make fundamental mistakes in thinking. The illogical forms of thinking contributed in significant ways to both airline crashes – the first crash based on beliefs and untested assumptions and cognitive biases, and the second crash which was preventable if Boeing leaders were more aware of cognitive biases and did not defend themselves using varied forms of illogical thinking.

What are some of the significant learnings from this case? They are:

- Boeing metrics (sales, profits, stock price) are a driving factor for these tragedies.
- "Safety First" is marketing nonsense. Cannot trust Boeing – must verify.
- Pilots in emergency situations are overloaded with too much information too quickly. They get confused and cannot respond effectively except in rare cases.
- Need to continuously improve processes for timely and accurate information flow within company and between key stakeholders.
- Leaders should plan for things going wrong, not just things going right.

• • • •

From this four-part failure analysis, we can see the significant role that business strategy and leadership decision-making had in the tragic 737 Max crashes. Too often business is seen as a game, such as to "own the market" or find clever ways to increase sales or the stock price. Business is not a game, and failure is no joke. People's lives and livelihoods are at stake. Executives like being in leaderships position but dislike the responsibility of being a leader and doing the work that is required to become a more skilled and competent leader. It means doing the never-ending work of improving one's thinking, engaging stakeholders, and recognizing and responding to the facts and mistakes as quickly as possible, and not use excuses for inaction such as "we don't have budget for that," "we need more data," or "it's their fault."

Boeing's 737 Max failure was driven by leadership's desire to save money and make more money through conquest and exploit. It backfired in dramatic fashion and cost the lives of 346 people and everlasting grief for thousands of family members and friends. The 21-month grounding of the aircraft also caused injury to parts suppliers and communities where workers were laid off. In the hope of saving a few billion dollars in product development costs and pilot training expense for customers, Boeing will have to spend 20 to 50 billion dollars. They will primarily spend it on:

- Fixing MCAS and related problems
- Lawsuits from different parties
- Penalty payments to airlines
- Pay lost profit to airlines
- Pay lost wages to pilots
- Factory inventories
- New advertising campaigns
- Canceled 737 Max orders
- Lost sales
- Pilot training in simulators

Penny-wise, pound-foolish leadership thinking is another recurring theme in strategy failure analysis.

One of the things Boeing leadership desired most to avoid, pilot training in flight simulators, became the thing that Boeing must now do and pay for, and at a cost that greatly exceeds what it would have been if pilots were trained in the

MCAS system from the start. This strategy to save money and make more money cost Boeing five or ten times more than the planned savings in new aircraft development and pilot training. The 737 Max program return on investment will likely be forever negative and drag down the profitability of the entire 737 aircraft program.

Boeing's leaders had the money to satisfy customers' wants and needs the correct way, but they squandered it on share buy-backs ($40 billion from FY13 to FY 18) and large increases in annual dividends to shareholders (from $0.3 billion in 2012 to more than $1 billion in 2018). Boeing went from an engineering company making quality products to a finance company doubling the cash flow and tripling the stock price while manufacturing a continuous string of defective products since the early 2000s.

Leaders have greater responsibility than they imagine. Chapter 2 describes how most leaders are too focused on themselves and not others. They are self-regarding and company-regarding, not other-regarding of employees, customers, suppliers, and communities – until tragedy occurs. Then they care for the forgotten stakeholders. The Boeing 737 Max is not an isolated case of catastrophic business strategy failure resulting in death and destruction.

Examples are reported almost every day in periodicals such as *The Wall Street Journal*, based largely on strategies. But success-oriented senior leaders are likely to ignore these failures, assuming they even read the newspaper. Examples of injury and death abound. Here is an abridged list of strategy failure analysis cases that were studied where the consequences were most severe in terms of injury to humans or loss of life:

- BP Texas Refinery Explosion
- General Motors Ignition Switch
- Johnson & Johnson OTC Drug Recalls
- Peanut Corporation of America Salmonella Recall
- Synthes Bone Cement
- Takata Airbags
- New England Compounding Center Fungal Meningitis
- Morcellator Medical Device
- Detroit Lead Water
- Blue Bell Ice Cream Listeria
- Grenfell Tower Fire
- Pacific Gas and Electric Wildfires
- Opioid Epidemic
- Morandi Bridge Failure
- Vale Mining Disaster
- Johnson & Johnson Baby Powder
- Fisher-Price Rock 'N Play Baby Sleeper
- COVID-19 Response Failure

These are merely the newsworthy strategy failures; the ones that make headlines. Similar strategy failures, though perhaps less injurious or deadly, happen in mid- and small-size businesses as well. Failed strategies of a less deadly nature have also been analyzed including Airbus A380 development, General Motors bankruptcy, Mylan epinephrine auto-injector, Wells Fargo fraud, varied accounting scandals, electricity deregulation, privatizing public assets, government tax breaks for technology companies, and others. A common theme among these failures is that which leaders seek most to avoid most ends up being the very thing that happens. It is a remarkably consistent pattern.

The most significant learning from the aggregate of strategy failure analyses is this:

Leaders' critical thinking skills are poor. The thing that leaders are the most confident about – analysis, logical thinking, and decision-making – are the things they should be the least confident about. Leaders' information processing abilities are highly error-prone and must be improved.

Beliefs and untested assumptions, cognitive biases, and illogical thinking are simply part of being human. However, the consequences of such unquestioning faith and undisciplined and uncritical reasoning are far greater when one is in a senior leadership position. How and why does that happen to leaders? Go back and re-read Chapters 1 and 2. The answer to the question will be very clear. Then read Chapter 3 again.

Are there other patterns of interest that come from analyzing strategy failures? Data was collected over a ten-year period to determine if discernable patterns existed with respect to cognitive bias and illogical thinking among the business leaders who were involved in failed strategies. The results were unexpected. Figure 3-1 shows the distribution of cognitive biases:

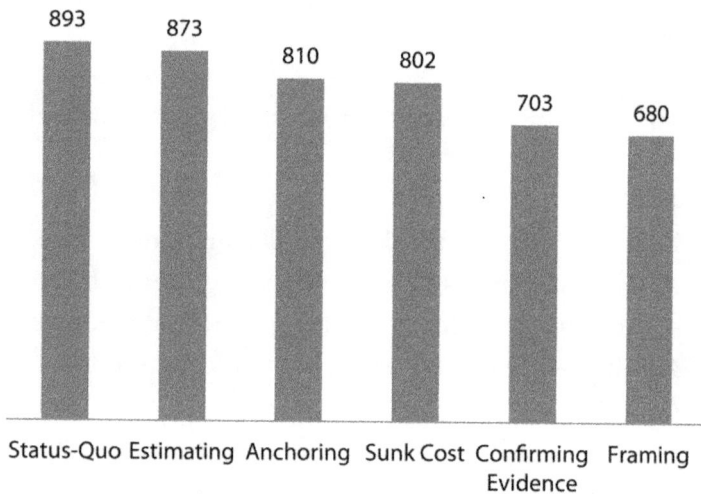

Figure 3-1. Distribution of cognitive biases (total number of occurrences identified in failure analysis cases studied).

It is clear that no one cognitive bias stands out. Cognitive biases occur in combination with one another. The lessons to learn from Figure 3-1 are:

- Despite talk of change, leaders prefer status quo
- Leaders are bad at estimating
- Leaders are easily anchored
- Leaders stick to their decisions
- Leaders ignore evidence that contradicts their views

The cognitive biases shown in Figure 3-1 are generally present in senior leaders' daily thinking and decision-making. They are part of the everyday lived experiences of workers in organizations and cause constant consternation among those who interact with senior leaders. In addition to figuring prominently in strategy failure, leaders' cognitive biases embed a measure of complacency in the company.

Figure 3-2 shows the distribution of illogical thinking:

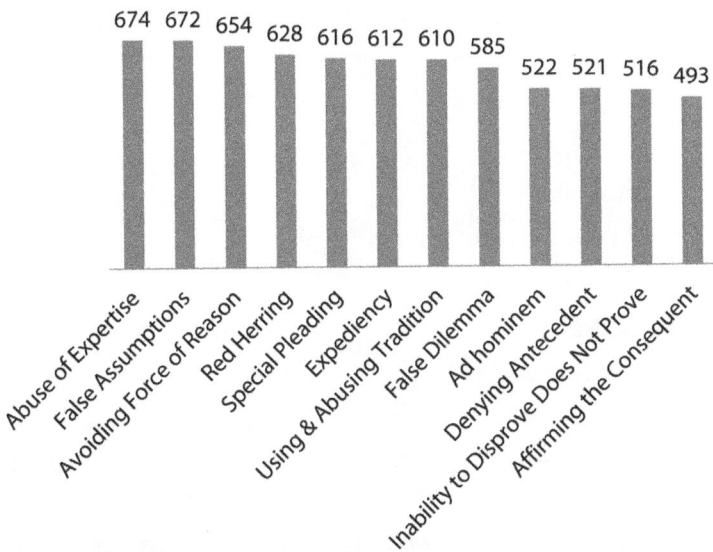

Figure 3-2. Distribution of illogical thinking (total number of occurrences identified in failure analysis cases studied).

It is clear that no single form of illogical thinking stands out. Illogical thinking occurs in combination. It too is ever-present in persons who occupy senior leadership positions and further instills complacency and the status quo.

The lessons to learn from Figure 3-2 are:

- People in power abuse expertise
- Leaders assume something is true without being sure that it is
- Leaders avoid the force of reason (they ignore facts)
- Red herring is used to evade responsibility
- Special pleading is used to strengthen one's position

There are other forms of illogical thinking that are evident in the cases studied [4]. Depending on the strategy failure, they may or may not be significant:

- Simplistic reasoning
- Strawman
- Avoiding conclusions
- Misclassification
- Reductionism
- Equivocation

None of the leaders involved in catastrophic strategy failure are uneducated or stupid. But they did have major blind spots that they could not overcome. Indeed, that is a difficult thing to do because the blind spots are deeply embedded in the role and function of being a senior leader. One such blind spot is a preference for opinion- or experience-based (self or others) problem-solving, riddled as it is with bad thinking and dismissal of real-world examples of failure (e.g., "that won't happen to us"). This is obviously inferior to fact-based structured problem-solving methods.

It reinforces the idea that formal strategy failure analysis should be prominent in business school education and in corporate leadership development programs. Formal strategy failure analysis provides needed real-world context and human impact that produces the type of learning experience that people remember and put into leadership practice. These results clearly indicate that different criteria are needed for selecting and promoting leaders, and that leaders, if they are true to their rhetoric about fiduciary responsibility, need to do the work required to become more capable and competent. They need to produce evidence of good thinking.

Cognitive biases come from preconceptions that leaders have about various economic, social, political, historical, philosophical, business, legal, and spiritual matters [5]. Preconceptions are baseline theories of what one believes to be true. Cognitive biases are the fitting of information to one's preconceptions and are thus subsequent to preconceptions (see Note 5). Both preconceptions and cognitive biases usually go untested; their truth is based on faith and are thus huge blind spots. The difficulty is that senior leadership teams generally share the same plenitude of preconceptions and related cognitive biases, which results in a reality that is different from the facts. This, coupled with the rank and grade in hierarchies, means that both poor (illogical) thinking and a lack of diversity in thinking are commonplace – yet decisions are certified by the group as sound. Strategy development and execution, and decision-making generally, are thus continually exposed to a high risk of failure.

The ubiquity of lazy and uncritical thinking means that some of the things that leaders cherish the most – social status, power, political influence, reputability, success, honor, dignity, and personal wealth – are at greatest risk. But the risk is either unknown or dismissed as a remote possibility. The 18 business deadly strategy failures listed previously cause leaders to lose many of the things that they value the most, and in some cases their freedom as well due to civil or criminal conviction. The thing that leaders fear most ends up happening to them, wrought by penny-wise, pound-foolish business strategy and decision-making. It bears repeating. The most significant learning from the aggregate of strategy failure analyses is this:

Leaders' critical thinking skills are poor. The thing that leaders are the most confident about – analysis, logical thinking, and decision-making – are the things they should be the least confident about. Leaders' information processing abilities are highly error-prone and must be improved.

It is also worth revisiting the pages near the beginning of this chapter; the answers and questions related to strategy failure analysis and note that the Strategy Failure Analysis Method produces the required information. Whatever may be missing can be found in Chapters 1 and 2.

The list below summarizes additional learnings from some 70 strategy failure analyses performed to-date:

- Leaders make the same types of mistakes
- Leaders copy other leader's ideas and solutions to problems
- Leaders are not trained to recognize say-do inconsistencies, question their beliefs and test their assumptions, recognize and avoid cognitive biases, or understand the major forms of illogical thinking
- Leaders' success bias causes them to discount or ignore the both high and low probability failures
- Leaders do not apply scientific thinking to their problems
- Solutions that produced good results in the past are used again for future problems
- Leaders are unwilling to experiment; therefore, there is little competition among ideas
- Conservatism reduces creativity in problem-solving
- Leaders trust their gut more than they trust the facts
- Leaders are unwilling to accept ownership and responsibility for problems, preferring instead to blame and scapegoat others
- Unrealistic targets set by leaders make them closed-minded to recognizing and correcting problems
- Leaders ignore lower-level people who possess the facts of the situation
- Leaders do not respect the experience, knowledge, and wisdom of lower-level people
- Leaders are too absorbed in pecuniary machinations
- Leaders' preference for zero-sum outcomes marginalizes key stakeholder who would be willing to offer help and guidance

- Injury to humans and loss of life are, at best, in the background of leadership thinking and decision-making
- Shared preconceptions, cognitive biases, and illogical thinking sow future problems
- Successful strategies are more the result of luck than intelligence, careful planning, or skilled execution

Leadership is a profession with serious consequences. It is not war or a sporting game, or an open field for conquest and exploit. As with anyone who is judged to be a "professional," leaders must undergo continuous training and development. An obvious corrective action is to train and coach senior leaders to have a better balance of success- and failure-orientation and to be more focused on the facts and lead more by the facts than by right or by gut. Leaders must learn to question their beliefs test their assumptions (preconceptions), learn the common cognitive biases and the major forms of illogical thinking.

Perhaps most of all, leaders should be curious and study the business strategy failures of other organizations. There is an adage that goes something like this:

Intelligent people learn from their mistakes.
Wise people learn from the mistakes of others.

Most senior leaders fall prey to the mistaken view that failure by another company or organization in a different industry or in a different country has no bearing on them or the company. On the contrary, they should be extremely interested in any major business failure because there is much to learn from it that can be applied to their work as leaders. For example, BPs Gulf of Mexico (Deepwater Horizon) oil spill may seem irrelevant to the leader of a technology company. But think again. A key learning – beyond human death and injury, deadly impact on marine life, and loss of livelihood for those who make their living from the sea – the worst that could happen did happen. What caused the oil spill will be similar to what can cause the worst to happen to any company. The disaster occurred because of a requirement by leaders to save time and a few million dollars, which, in turn, blocked information coming from lower levels that warned of problems, and ended up costing BP some 65 billion dollars. Leaders will be more adept at avoiding problems if they recognize faulty decision-making as the rule, not as the exception.

However, senior leaders do not easily yield to new ways of thinking and doing things because they do not have to. They can do as they please, and accountability for failure runs downhill. This destructive pattern of behavior must be arrested. Conducting failure analyses on a regular basis, individually and as a leadership team, will greatly deepen their understanding of the causes of failure and help them identify and implement countermeasures to help ensure major failures do not occur. Senior leaders must become more curious to learn about failure, across industries and countries, to learn from the mistakes of others. The fiduciary and non-fiduciary responsibilities of leadership require leaders to accept as part of their duty to understand, in lurid detail, how others fail and ensure that such outcomes do not occur. The Strategy Failure Analysis Method should become a routine leadership development activity in organizations. Consider that instead of being educated to succeed, leaders have inadvertently been educated in school and on-the-job to fail. Hence, the need for strategy failure analysis.

· · · ·

So, what else can be done (see Note 6)? Business strategy, being simply copied from other leaders (CEO's Wealth Creation Playbook, Table 1-1), is assumed to be right and good (see Note 7). Business leaders, being success-oriented, are attentive when the strategy succeeds but they ignore the strategy when it fails. The strategy is assumed to be intrinsically good and failure is assumed to be the result of poor execution. As such, there is no reason to test the strategy to determine if it is sound or unsound. It is a mistake to assume a strategy is automatically good because other leaders use it. It is also a mistake to assume that failure is due to poor execution. A smarter approach would be to test a strategy after it is formulated, but before it is deployed, to identify intrinsic defects and make corrections. A strategy testing tool is needed.

The Strategy Failure Analysis Method can be reformulated into a predictive tool to avoid future failures. It can be used proactively as a structured problem-*avoiding* method – the problem being how to avoid failure in strategy development and execution. The fundamental task is to test the strategy to see if it contains the seeds of failure that would be likely to grow and eventually propagate. Strategy can be put to an acid test to determine its likelihood of success. If it fails the acid test, then the strategy must be reformulated or abandoned. If it passes the acid test, likely with numerous corrections, then it can proceed. What does such a test look like? What follows is a description of a two-part method used in a workshop setting to test a strategy.

Strategy Acid Test Method – Part One

The first step of the Strategy Acid Test Method (SATM) is to concisely articulate the strategy. The next step is to identify why the strategy is necessary. The third step is to identify how and when each stakeholder will be impacted by the strategy. The final step is to identify beliefs and untested assumptions (preconceptions) upon which the strategy is based. Are the assumptions true or false, valid or invalid?

This part of the acid test will give a fuller picture of the strategy, its rationale, and its expected impact on varied people and organizations. To the greatest extent possible, stakeholders should not be subjected to zero-sum outcomes characteristic of conquest and exploit. If that happens, the strategy will need further analysis and refinement so that it results in mutually beneficial outcomes.

Strategy Acid Test Method – Part Two

The first step is to identify the cognitive biases that are embedded in the strategy. The second step is to identify the illogical thinking that is embedded in the strategy. The third step, based on the findings of the previous two steps, is to identify proactive countermeasures to take to help avoid or eliminate the possibility of failure.

Having completed Part One and Part Two, the strategy can then be refined and improved to eliminate its many built-in faults. It could also include a formal root cause analysis examining the need for change, which may turn out to be based on faulty thinking. Or it could include identification of weaknesses in functional processes that will inhibit achieving the strategy. There could also be a short checklist of considerations to review before key decisions are made.

The overall objective of strategy testing can be thought of this way: Build your strategy and then tear it down. Do it three or four times. This process will identify weaknesses that need to be corrected before strategy becomes fixed and later executed. It requires leaders to not be beholden to a favored strategy. Instead, they must allow the process of strategy acid testing to shape and improve the strategy.

The final step is a "Go" or "No-Go" decision. If "No-Go," then the strategy can be reformulated and re-tested for defects using the Two-Part method. Or the strategy could be abandoned because the Two-Part method might reveal that it is unnecessary. It could be that other, more important actions need to be taken internally. If the strategy goes forward, then there can be a periodic review of its progress in relation to the acid test documentation to examine whether the strategy is succeeding as planned or starting to stumble. Corrective actions could then be taken, but always screened for beliefs and untested assumptions, cognitive biases, and illogical thinking.

Please reflect on the wisdom of Henry Ford [6]:

> "A man who cannot think is not an educated man however many college degrees he may have acquired. Thinking is the hardest work any one can do – which is probably the reason why we have so few thinkers... If education consisted in warning the young student away from some of the false theories on which men have tried to build, so that he may be saved the loss of the time in finding out by bitter experience, its good would be unquestioned. An education which consists of signposts indicating the failure and the fallacies of the past doubtless would be very useful...the best that education can do for a man is to... teach him how to think."

Formal education, generally, and business education, particularly, is not good at "warning the young student away from some of the false theories on which men have tried to build." On-the-job training is worse in the sense that runs in the opposite direction – it avoids the warnings and instead focuses on success, which unintentionally embeds the seeds of failure. Skepticism is cast aside because it is unbusinesslike. It is vulgar and offensive to people high in status and who possess great power and wealth.

This book has provided readers with the "signposts indicating the failure and the fallacies of the past," and in some small measure it has "[taught you] how to think." But it does not end there. Senior leaders must do the work to recover their lost ability to think critically so that they do not have to find out by "bitter experience." They can instead learn from the mistakes of other leaders (see Note 8). It is both more efficient and more informative to do that. More efficient because it is the least waste of time and effort and more informative because it is easier to see the mistakes of others than one's own mistakes.

Intelligent people learn from their mistakes.
Wise people learn from the mistakes of others.

Is being intelligent good enough for you (Figure 3-3)? The job of senior leader requires wisdom as well as intelligence.

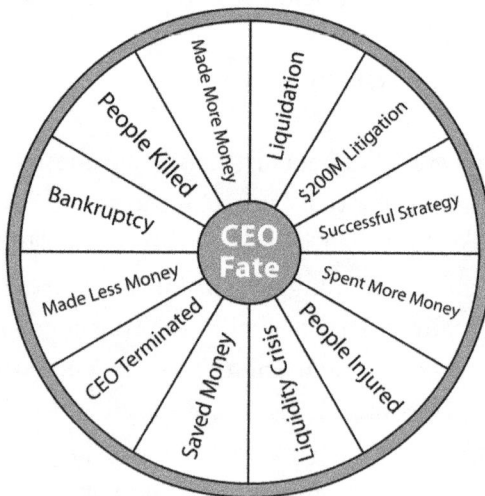

Figure 3-3. The Wheel of Fortune includes very real probability of great misfortune, where unfavorable things usually happen in combination with one another.

Notes

1. Blaming and scapegoating is a common feature in business. It stems from the cult of victimhood, wherein responsibility and accountability are more applicable to others than it is to top leaders.

2. The first author (Emiliani) joined academia in 1999 after working 15 years in industry. The business school in which he taught made extensive use of the case study method in its graduate degree programs. The case studies invariably described some type of business success story. Almost never was failure discussed, in part because of a lack of case study material on this subject. Case study writers long recognized that access for case writing was contingent on them saying good things about the companies and leaders that they studied. As a result, both the Harvard case study teaching method and the learning that students gain from it are plainly corrupt – the former due to the near ceaseless focus on success [7] and the latter for not providing the wisdom to students that Henry Ford urged educators to impart (see page 87). Having worked in industry and both a witness and participant in failures as worker and leader in engineering, manufacturing, and supply chain management, it was apparent that business school education did not accurately represent the "real world." Business periodicals such as *The Wall Street Journal* and *The Financial Times* publish stories of business failures, large and small, every day, yet the focus of business school education is success. This is unlike engineering education, which better balances analysis of success and failure. So, based on Emiliani's engineering

education, his work as an engineer and with engineering failure analysis, and management experience, he set about to develop a new methodology for analyzing business failures: strategy, bankruptcies, defective products, and shoddy services. These are common occurrences and should be studied because, as is often said, "You learn more from mistakes than success." Yet, there is little to learn from failures if they are not carefully studied. The failure analysis method presented here, continuously improved over a 16-year period, has been used in a graduate master's degree program to educate students about the varied forms of business failure and to teach them the failure analysis methodology. The course was first taught in the summer of 2004. Since then, some 70 failure cases have been studied, with most students, who are working professionals like you, saying it was the best course they ever had in their graduate program of study. The confluence of real-world situation and structured analysis makes for a great and memorable learning experience. The question, always, is: "Do you put what you learn into practice?" If yes, expensive and embarrassing failures will be mostly avoided. If not, expensive and embarrassing failures will be mostly repeated.

3. The source material is collected from various business periodicals. These neutral organizations report on failures by engaging first-hand sources of information and analyzing related documents. The information produced is of a quality and quantity sufficient to produce accurate failure analyses and to identify practical countermeasures. In high-profile cases such as the 737 Max, formal government investigations arrive at the same conclusions as that

produced by the Strategy Failure Analysis Method described in this chapter [8]. One might think that failure analysis would be better if one were to interact directly with those who had a hand in the failure. The convergence of the Strategy Failure Analysis Method and third-part failure analysis (government) shows that it is not necessary for the scope of failure under consideration (i.e., strategy and management decision-making).

4. No doubt senior leaders will claim that they do not have time to read and digest so many pages. It will always be more the case that they do not want to do it rather than they cannot do it. They naturally prefer the continuity afforded by "business-as-usual." If working professional students can find time to do the reading with the pressure of work and family life, so can senior leaders. Their job is to avoid failure by raising their intelligence. And senior leaders have the added advantage of delegating their tasks so that they can focus on strategy failure analysis to become more capable and competent.

5. Preconceptions, cognitive biases, and illogical thinking are partly the result of leaders being physically and mentally distant from the actual work, and an unwillingness to engage workers where they work to understand the facts of the situation. This problem is the result of senior leaders wishing to preserve or enhance their own social status above the interests of the company or its workers. Leaders possess the social status, power, political influence, reputability, success, honor, dignity, and personal wealth whether they interact with workers or not. The far bigger

problem that senior leaders have concern over is the possibility of being embarrassed – an appearance problem that is a tiny, short-lived personal price to pay for avoiding catastrophic failure and the life-long embarrassment that goes with that. Furthermore, the nonproductive work of leaders above the level of middle manager gives them an abundance of time to think of ways to impinge on the productive work of workers.

6. Post-737 Max disasters, Boeing's new structural reforms and compliance programs do not prevent faulty thinking by top leaders in their future search for pecuniary gain [9].

7. One must admit, even if only in secret, that bill of expense for top leadership is surprisingly high given that nearly all the strategies listed in Table 1-1 to increase pecuniary gain were worked out long ago. Furthermore, such decisions can be made by almost anyone less skilled in the practical art and science of pecuniary gain (all they need is the list), and these strategies are invariably delegated to others for their execution. So, there is neither originality of thought nor toil of work to justify the great expense of top leadership. That is not to say that senior leaders should not be well compensated, but it is to say that compensation should not so greatly exceed the actual value of the mundane service rendered.

8. The first author (Emiliani) wishes to acknowledge and thank his graduate students for their meticulous work and insights on the many strategy failure analysis cases, some of which is presented in aggregate in this chapter.

References

[1] Emiliani, B. (2020), *Irrational Institutions: Business, Its Leaders, and The Lean Movement*, Cubic LLC, South Kingstown, Rhode Island

[2] Hart-Smith, L.J. (2001), "Out-Sourced Profits – The Cornerstone of Successful Subcontracting," Boeing Paper MDC 00K0096, presented at Boeing Third Annual Technical Excellence (BATE) Symposium, St. Louis, Missouri, 14-15 February (Note: The title of the paper is sarcastic. The intent of the paper is to criticize the increase in outsourcing that Boeing leaders were aiming for in aircraft development and production in the early 2000s).

[3] Tang, C., Zimmerman, J., and Nelson, M (2009), "Managing New Product Development and Supply Chain Risks: The Boeing 787 Case," *Supply Chain Forum: An International Journal*, Vol. 10, No. 2, pp. 74-86

[4] McInerny, D. (2005), *Being Logical: A Guide to Good Thinking*, Random House, New York, New York. See also https://en.wikipedia.org/wiki/List_of_fallacies

[5] Emiliani, B. (2018), *The Triumph of Classical Management Over Lean Management: How Tradition Prevails and What to Do About It*, Cubic LLC, South Kingstown, Rhode Island

[6] Ford, H. with Crowther, S. (1922), *My Life and Work*, with S. Crowther, Doubleday, Page & Co., Garden City, New York, pages 247 and 248

[7] Thomas, P. (2021), "Covid-19 Case Studies Make Their Way Into M.B.A. Curricula," *The Wall Street Journal*, 6 January, https://www.wsj.com/articles/covid-19-case-studies-make-their-way-into-m-b-a-curricula-11609938003, accessed 6 January 2021

[8] Majority Staff of the Committee on Transportation and Infrastructure (2020), "Final Committee Report: The Design, Development & Certification of the Boeing 737 MAX," The House Committee on Transportation and Infrastructure, September, https://transportation.house.gov/committee-activity/boeing-737-max-investigation, accessed 1 January 2021

[9] Tokar, D. (2021), "Prosecutors Credited Boeing for Compliance, Organizational Reforms," *The Wall Street Journal*, 15 January, https://www.wsj.com/articles/prosecutors-credited-boeing-for-compliance-organizational-reforms-11610723642, accessed 15 January 2021

4

Strategic Choices: Copy or Create

Strategic Choices: Copy or Create

Does it still make sense today to talk about strategy? Or does today's liquid, interconnected, and global world only require the ability to adapt and seize opportunities from wherever they come? Is strategy to be relegated to history books or business cases that academics and business students are so fond of? Have today's markets spelled the end of strategy? Could it be that the continued focus on efficiency and cost cutting has reduced the concern of senior leaders and entrepreneurs to minimum viable requirements for prosperity from one day to the next? If strategy is to remain a useful concept and practice in business, then there needs to be a reexamination of the intent of strategy and the process by which strategy is typically developed.

Defining a strategy requires both art and science. That is, imagination (art) of a possible future, of a different or better state than the current state, and science, that is, a capacity for rigorous analysis, evaluation of possible options, and the ability to create a plan, which, based on cause-and-effect, can define the steps necessary to achieve the defined objectives. The academic and consulting worlds have produced an enormous number of case studies. They have analyzed strategy dynamics and tactics and produced models and templates of winning strategies. These works, focused on the art of strategy, are produced unremittingly and in profusion. Yet, doubts emerge upon examination of actual results. If the secrets to a winning strategy have been so well codified, then why are there so few success stories directly attributable to strategy? And most strategy success stories are based on the same general strategy, one that moves in the direction of monopoly or similar anticompetitive behavior.

Defining a unique strategy is difficult because most academic and consulting studies of strategy are not scientific. That is, they have a useful explanatory value – they explain the past – but they have no predictive value; they do not predict the future. They are good stories, and they help people understand the strategy and outcomes. While educational, they have less value in terms of inspiring people to think in fresh ways and build something new. A profusion of models, templates, and lists have been produced to structure existing thought processes, but they produce little in the way of new ideas. It takes imagination and creativity to produce new ideas, and the preconceptions and cognitive biases associated with business and strategy largely prevent that.

Most models and templates arise from the analysis of successful cases. They tell you that if you apply the model you will be successful. But the model is precisely the product of the analysis of a successful case, so the reasoning is circular. Furthermore, models and templates, when well-constructed, are frames that must be filled with ideas whose source is informed by preconceptions. While they create a structure that helps to think in a more disciplined way, they do not generate practical and specific breakthroughs in thinking applicable to the company or market. No model or template can create what is not there. Ideas are what make the difference in the practical reality of business.

It follows that to conceive a unique strategy, it is necessary to first have ideas; a lot of ideas followed by a thoughtful synthesis of ideas to decide on preferred directions. This synthesis combines customer needs with the desired business and economic results and the values and aspirations of those who lead the company, those who work in the company, and those who buy from the company. The strategy must be a more scientific selection from varied choices and priorities, which, in turn, specify preferred directions compared to others.

Figure 4-1. Leonardo da Vinci's Vitruvian Man (L'uomo vitruviano, ca. 1490) representing human beings thinking about the many choices that they can make.

Another reason why defining a unique strategy difficult is due to the lack of leadership courage to abandon the solutions of the past – the common recipes for success. Most leaders adopt the same or similar formula that others have used [1]. The problem lies in the inability to abandon the formula because it is the idea of a respected business leader, the idea of the company founder, or reluctance to do something different. Strategy is more consistent with habit than creativity. It is a habit of not thinking independently and thus a habit of following others and copying (see Note 1). And doing so not truly knowing if others were actually successful because success stories are typically inflated and problems discounted or buried, whether recounted first-hand or by second- or third-hand sources such as business news periodicals. Thus, habits, while at times useful, can at other times be a great handicap [2]:

"Habit is the most infamous of illnesses because it makes us accept any accident, any pain, any death. For habit we live next to odious people, you learn to carry the chains and to be subjected to injustice, to suffer, you resign to pain, to solitude, to all. Habit is the most merciless of poisons because it seeps in slowly, silently and it grows slowly fostering on our unawareness, and when we discover we have it on us every move is conditioned, no medicine exists than can heal us."

In a world where everyone does the same things, whether they are all very good or all mediocre, the general result is homogeneity and undifferentiation. It is a general problem in the business world that academic studies, trade magazine articles, books by retired business leaders, and workshops promoted as innovative are, in reality, the usual old ideas with a new name or perhaps some small variation added to it. The uncomfortable truth we do not like to confront is that there is very little real innovation. That is because innovation is hard to produce due to the restrictions we voluntarily place on ourselves by not questioning our numerous preconceptions and a steadfast unwillingness to be different because of its high social costs.

Creating and innovating requires great effort, energy, and courage which can be a mentally and emotionally exhausting process. It is much easier to accept the known path rather than to try to take a new path. It is more difficult to abandon habits, preconceptions, cognitive biases, and illogical thinking than it is to develop new ideas. Consequently, leaders and companies become prisoners of their successful past and have great difficulty reinventing themselves as times change and as customers and their needs change. So, leaders continue along with their old recipe for success, aware of the changing world but unable to respond to it effectively or in time. Eventually, senior leaders face a crisis when they discover one day that their sales or their market share is disappearing.

There are rare cases in which the disaster occurs suddenly, but in most cases the signals of impending crisis are weak. The company begins to lose a customer here, then another there. The product or service that was supposed to relaunch the company does not work as predicted. Sales begin to decline slowly. It looks more like noise than signal. But then profits start to fall continuously because, to increase sales and maintain market share, prices must be lowered. Employees in important positions, sensing a growing crisis, leave to take jobs elsewhere. A new strategy is developed in haste, one that almost surely consists of old ideas. If it is successful, it is more due to luck than exceptional creative thinking and skilled execution. If it is unsuccessful, the company is put up for sale to the highest bidder. Neglecting the weak signals and the temporal dimension – time – means leaders have difficulty making necessary adjustments to avoid a crisis and enter the spiral of declining sales and profits. This, in turn, leads to a chronic lack of resources that delays recovery or impedes investment in new directions.

Some companies subscribe to the "do it all" strategy, which is not a strategy. It is an inability to make choices. Thus, they pursue business and product development policies that are inconsistent, fragmented, and conflicting. In doing so they create unmanageable complexity that results in innumerable problems for which those lower in the hierarchy get blamed. A variation on the "do it all" strategy is the use of slogans-as-strategy such as "we put customers first" or "do whatever customers want." Indeed, for whom is the customer not important? No customer, no cash, no company. While such statements are trivial, they are easily forgotten by leaders in their aggressive pursuit of pecuniary gain. Customer slogans-as-strategy are cover for leaders' absence of vision and refusal to think and act in new ways. These statements lack originality and do not represent any grand strategy because they are so easily subverted by self-serving corporate interests. As such, platitudes offer no vision for the future and they are likely to cause great confusion in the lower ranks because they are a wellspring of "say-do" inconsistencies.

There is no model or template that can replace the generation of new ideas. It comes from within through imagination and engagement with the environment of customer, the problem they need solved, and their desired experience, whether it exists now or planned as something to be created. Leaders are free to copy common business strategies, and, in some cases, it might be the right thing to do. Such a choice cannot be ruled out in advance, but its limitations should be clear. Occam's razor, or the law of parsimony, is the problem-solving principle that the simplest explanation is usually the right explanation. In a world that is unpredictable, uncontrollable, and chaotic, it is necessary to have mindsets and methods that are flexible and ready to react to changing situations. And this is where adaptability, imagination, and creativity find their full application. Often, these qualities and capabilities are inspired by analogies to things that may or may not be a useful guide for how to think.

Strategic thinking and, more generally, the way people think is strongly influenced or inspired by the type of metaphor used. In business and strategy, the most common metaphors are military (war) [3, 4] and sports [5, 6]. However, business is not war and competitors are not the enemy to defeat (see Note 2). Competitors are part of the ecosystem that others depend on for survival. Without competitors, complacency sets in and hardens. It creates an invisible disadvantage that slowly builds and will one day emerge and become obvious. Military metaphor, fighting the competition, is the wrong focus. Customers – gaining new customers and retaining existing customers and being adaptable to changes in customer wants and needs – is the point of focus (see Note 3).

Challenges in business have different origins. New technologies, new business models, alternative products, or profound changes in the habits of customers easily upset entire markets. Usually, competitors bent on war, conquest and exploit, miss the weak signals indicative of changes in the customer wants and needs. Much of this occurs because leaders typically refuse to hear or acknowledge bad news. High fidelity information, usually originating from lower in the organization closer to customers, is filtered in ways that eliminate weak signals that have the potential to upend the leader's strategy, production, product development, or other plans.

The sports metaphor is also incorrect. Business is not a game whose objective it is to thoroughly vanquish or humiliate one's opponent. Yet there is a strong appetite for this metaphor. Professional sports coaches share their methods and tips on how to best manage teams and how to create winning teams. The public fascination with famous coaches, players, and the many books they write helps to embed the comparison of a company to a professional sports team and the requirement for zero-sum outcomes – winning. As much as the sports metaphor may inspire and perhaps have points of interest, a company is not a sports team and employees are not players. Managers do not act as coaches because the organization of business conforms to military hierarchy. Today, most managers do not know the details of the work they oversee, having never done it themselves, so they cannot coach effectively. So instead, they just tell people what to do, absent the learning that coaching in sports seeks to impart.

Two things that seem to be similar are not exactly the same. For example, professional sports teams have a small number of players, whereas companies, the kinds with formalized strategic plans, typically have hundreds or thousands of employees. In professional sports teams, there are aspects of relationship and cooperation, just as there is in a company. But the small size of the professional sports team facilitates the exchange of ideas, experiences, and behaviors. In a company, the structures, processes, procedures, policies, internal politics, and arrangement and distribution of resources greatly complicate the processes of employee interaction and the quality of interactions. Furthermore, games in sports have clear rules, a clearly defined objective (win the game), and a clearly identified competitor (the opposing team). In sports, games last two to three hours, whereas business is ongoing. Winning in sports is well-defined, whereas winning in business can be defined any way that a leader chooses, including when one has obviously lost. Business is much more complex, where sometimes the concept of rules, competitors, goals, and winning are blurred, inconsistent, or incomprehensible.

The metaphors we use profoundly influence the creation of mental maps that condition our way of thinking and that may not represent reality in the most useful way. Therefore, we must be careful not to invoke military or sports metaphors beyond the facts of the matter and make comparisons that are inaccurate or invalid. Many thousands of people have participated in workshops led by famous professional sports coaches and military leaders. The question is, why does business not evolve and get better? It is because these metaphors and the resulting books and workshops, while perhaps fun and interesting, merely reinforce the status quo. Their common feature is to copy, not to think. They offer new-sounding things, but little or nothing is truly new. In fact, these metaphors, rooted in exploit and conquest, can get companies into big trouble (see Chapter 3).

What does offer something new is the metaphor of Nature and its means and methods for solving problems and navigating survival. Nature does not filter out bad news or weak signals. It adapts as circumstances change in a complex and dynamic world. Nature processes information with less error than humans do. Strategic choices are grounded in the fact-based material world, and progress is dependent on creativity and innovation and the choices therein. Leaders vastly underestimate or ignore employees' abilities, at all levels, to think of creative and innovative solutions to problems – and the possibility that they could think of strategies that are superior to those developed by leaders because they are less burdened by the social obligations of leadership and the preconceptions and cognitive biases that constrain senior leaders (see Note 4).

Notes

1. The habit of following others and copying others is rooted in social learning that produces strong biases (preferences) that are both conformist and emulative of role models. Leaders' loss of creative and innovative instincts stems from the routinized and impersonal nature of leadership generally, and particularly in large corporations. This is aided by the focus on rights and privileges associated with ownership, as opposed to serving the broader interests of stakeholders, especially customers.

2. It is more accurate to say that the enemy to defeat is not the competition, but one's self – one's altered view of reality from the top of the hierarchy, beliefs and untested assumptions, say-do inconsistencies, preconceptions, cognitive biases, and illogical thinking. That is the ever-present enemy that leaders should focus on and seek to eliminate to the extent possible. For it is these that distract all employees from their customers and produces an unremitting self-regarding, rather than other-regarding focus.

3. Who among us has not had a long-term relationship with a company whose product or service continuously fails to meet our needs in some important way? We are clearly unhappy with those companies that place their interests above customers' interests and would seek a better alternative if one were available. The march towards monopoly and other anticompetitive behavior illustrates that senior leaders would rather be served by customers

than serve customers. However, leaders must not to fall into the "do it all" or "do whatever customers want" traps. The former results in loss of focus and needless complexity, while the latter can take one towards Amazon-like anticompetitive practices (see Chapter 2, reference 3).

4. The logic of leadership is to view business as a financial enterprise while the logic of lower-level employees is to view business as a customer satisfaction enterprise (i.e., happy customers). The former view leads to financial innovation and associated complexity (often some form of sabotage of another party's interests), while the latter view leads to customer innovation and associated simplicity. Given that, in most cases, business strategy is mere copying of someone else's strategy, involving zero creative or innovative thinking, why not allow others who are closer to the customer to develop strategy or provide inputs that are incorporated into strategy? This can result in a better understanding of the strategy by employees, greater buy-in, and more focused execution. The people at the top are not the only ones with brains that can think, though they are usually far more constrained than others lower in the hierarchy.

References

[1] Porter, M. (1998), *Competitive Strategy: Techniques for Analyzing Industries and Competitors*, Free Press, New York, New York

[2] Fallaci, O. (2014), *Un Uomo*, BUR Biblioteca Univerzale Rizzoli, Milan, Italy

[3] McNeilly, M. (2011), *Sun Tzu and the Art of Business: Six Strategic Principles for Managers*, Oxford University Press, New York, New York

[4] Willink, J. (2017), *Extreme Ownership: How U.S. Navy SEALs Lead and Win,* St. Martin's Press, New York, New York

[5] Westerbeek, H, and Smith, A. (2005), *Business Leadership and the Lessons from Sport*, Palgrave Macmillan, New York, New York

[6] Cuban, M. (2013), *How to Win at the Sport of Business: If I Can Do It, You Can Do It*, Diversion Books, New York, New York

5

Imagination and Creativity

Imagination and Creativity

The book *The Martian* by Andy Weir [1] is a fictionalized account of an astronaut stranded on Mars after his fellow astronauts left the planet believing he was dead. The book, and Hollywood film, describe how Mark Watney applied his spirit, energy, imagination, and creativity as an explorer to survive. With no way to communicate to Earth or spaceships, he must figure out how to survive for as long as possible with limited oxygen, water, and food. A series of calamities put ever-greater pressure on astronaut Watney to use his imagination and creativity to survive against seemingly impossible odds until help arrives.

The Martian is obviously not a story of how innovative a company was, how brilliant an entrepreneur was, or how skilled a CEO was. It is a science fiction story that teaches readers about imagination, creativity, ingenuity, and problem-solving. And so, it is a book about strategy, one that has great explanatory value for understanding what humans are capable of when faced with a big challenge. There is hidden power in this story in part because it describes both success and failure under adverse conditions, even if it is only imagined.

During his isolation on Martian soil, Watney must solve a long series of problems and devise solutions in a dangerous and unforgiving environment. He must overcome various life-threatening difficulties and carefully consider the many constraints and limited resources. Sometimes Watney makes mistakes, but he owns his mistakes, and he learns from them. Being clear about *what not to do* is as fundamental as knowing *what to do* – the former being an important lesson to learn from Chapter 3, Strategy Failure Analysis.

Astronaut Watney uses an eight-step process to contend with problems he faces, each of which have varying levels of complexity:

1. Tries to understand what is happening
2. Imagines the outcome he needs to achieve
3. Generates and explores alternatives
4. Identifies the most promising course of action
5. Identifies the actions to be taken
6. Evaluates if he has the resources and means to do them
7. He takes action
8. And then he checks the result. If it is good, he proceeds with his plan for survival. Otherwise, he starts over and repeats the cycle.

Watney goes through all eight steps several times, solving the problem that presents itself each time, proceeding by trial and error after thinking about it for a while. Things frequently do not go as expected. Therefore, Watney must adapt and continuously change plans and objectives. But he never loses sight of his primary direction, survival, and the general direction or intended purpose, to get rescued.

The structured problem-solving process is Watney's key to survival. Strategy is a solution to one or more serious problems. How often are structured problem-solving processes used by senior leaders – themselves, not their delegates – to solve the problems such as that required by a strategy? Is it not more often *ad hoc*? If a structured problem-solving process is used, it always, somehow and to a great extent, is contaminated by faulty beliefs and untested assumptions, cognitive biases, and illogical thinking (see Note 1).

Table 5-1 summarizes the four phases of the eight-step problem-solving process that Watney used, but configured for use in problem-solving for the purpose of creating strategy – a plan for business survival.

Table 5-1: Strategy Problem-Solving

Problem-Solving Phase	Problem-Solving Steps
Thinking	1. Understand what is happening 2. Imagine outcomes you would like to achieve 3. Generate and explore multiple alternatives 4. Identify the most promising alternative
Planning	5. Identify the actions to be taken 6. Evaluate the availability of resources and means
Apply the Strategy Acid Test to analyze and refine the strategy	
Implementation	7. Take Action
Reflection	8. Check the result. If it is good, proceed with the plan. Otherwise start over and repeat the cycle.

The problem-solving process shown in Table 5-1 is not linear. The characteristics of a strategy that would generate new and original solutions requires moving back and forth through the various steps, following the development of a thought that imagines new paths instead of following ordinary or popular paths. Always try to understand and communicate each step of a complex problem visually, in pictures, by drawing simple sketches, clipping images from various sources, etc. Use as few words as possible. Do not create thick reports or lengthy presentations. Summarize the results of each step in one page that contains mostly sketches or images.

Changing circumstances continuously generate new problems that must be faced and solved just as they happen (see Note 2). Mark Watney does not have the luxury of doing as most companies do, which is to allow long lags between problem recognition and problem-solving. A company that operates in a competitive market must react to problems as they happen. Yet, in most companies, people get blamed for pointing out problems, and so problem recognition is delayed, sometimes by years. Watney must recognize and solve problems in real-time to survive. Senior leaders should do the same. Business leaders who can imagine themselves in Watney's shoes would take swift actions when problems arise.

Next, let's elaborate on the first stage of the eight-step problem-solving process (Thinking), as this is the most important step because it is a significant determinant of success or failure in the next three phases of the problem-solving process: Planning, Implementation, and Reflection.

1. Understand What is Happening

This implies knowing the situation in which one must operate; current analysis of the market, opportunities and challenges, and the many forces in play that may impact the future. A good strategy answers the classic questions: why, how, what, where, and who. The difficulty arises in defining the parameters of the problems and problem to be solved, neither of which are always clear. The problem that business strategy seeks to solve is a so-called "wicked-problem" in that it is messy and difficult to solve discretely with a single easy solution, despite efforts to do just that. Such shortcuts increase the risk of future trouble.

Experience in the field shows that many times neither the market nor the alternatives present are well known or explored. The only source of information are comments and observations reported in the company by salespeople who repeat what they have heard in interactions with customers or potential customers. The information thus obtained, although perhaps useful, usually does not represent anything novel and therefore must be used carefully in problem-solving because it can be contaminated by faulty beliefs and untested assumptions, cognitive biases, and illogical thinking. Therefore, in-depth market analysis means collecting information from multiple sources, especially those which contradict or refute established knowledge or understandings. Counterarguments are extremely useful for thinking through problems and developing a greater awareness of potential solutions.

2. Imagine What You Would Like to Obtain

Start asking questions and start dreaming. What do customers want now or what do you think they want in the future? Should you be in those markets? And in what way? What products or services can be offered? What kind of company do employees want it to be? What do they want to achieve? Many possible futures should be imagined and carefully evaluated.

3. Generate and Explore Seven Alternatives

We often hear the mantra "think out of the box." But it is not always clear which box we are in, which box we are talking about, what it contains inside, or how it is made (its structure). Assuming the contours and elements of the problem are well-defined, the most challenging part is the creation of possible alternatives. This is the moment for imagination and creativity; to think of seven or ten alternatives, not just one or two or three.

Generating seven alternatives is a much greater challenge than just one or two alternatives. Imagination is not used when the choice made is selected from the first few alternative that easily come to mind. Developing seven alternatives is essential to increase the chances of success. What can inspire imagination to expand the number of choices? Look to Nature, the arts, Leonardo [2], Harriet Tubman [3], Marie Curie [4], Mark Watney, or similar sources of inspiration. Or, sometimes one just has to think harder than ever before to squeeze out the necessary creativity. Remember to understand and communicate each step of a complex problem simply and visually.

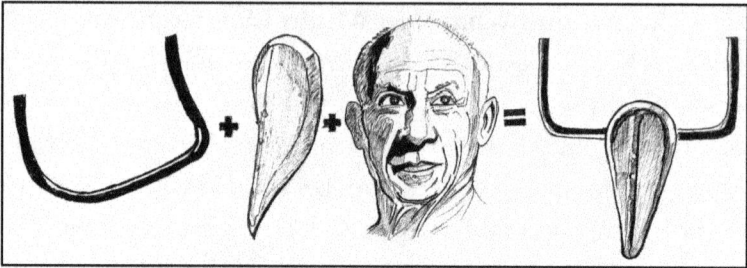

Figure 5-1. Example of creativity produced by combining common elements, bicycle handlebar and seat, in a novel way to produce a new result (Pablo Picasso's "Bulls Head,", 1942).

4. Identify the Most Promising Alternative

If the three previous steps have been carried out thoughtfully, it should now be possible to draw up a list of potential actions that must then be evaluated through both qualitative and quantitative analysis. Because quantitative analysis can generally produce whatever numbers one desires, it is especially important to carefully perform a qualitative analysis featuring rigorous critical thinking. To do this successfully, one must argue both sides of the case – for and against. The subroutine to this part of the problem-solving process are these four steps (see Note 3):

- Argument
- Counterargument
- Discussion
- Learning and improving

Be careful not to marginalize the counterarguments. If the process is carried through with integrity – no politics or hidden agendas – it will lead to a series of actions that are coherent in all their aspects. After the Thinking and Planning phases have been completed, apply the Strategy Acid Test Method (Chapter 3) to understand and correct weaknesses in the strategy.

Successful companies produce lots of ideas and put constructive pressure on people to think differently. The challenge is to make greater use of one's intelligence, whether at the senior level or at the working levels. While structured problem-solving methods can help, it is increasingly important to raise intelligence and build capabilities for quickly analyzing rapidly changing situations and developing original solutions in an evolutionary process that never ends. A way of thinking that creates new pathways for survival by developing the ability to maneuver thought (imagination, creativity, analysis) to become a truly strategic asset.

Mark Watney's survival story can be seen in this complementary way:

- Respect facts
- Relentless curiosity
- Careful observation
- Understand the details
- Think across boundaries of knowledge
- Use imagination to overcome difficulties

Watney was in dire circumstances, so he was forced to think creatively based on the facts of the matter. Most business leaders do not think of themselves or the company as being in dire circumstances and often wave off inconvenient facts. The leader is wealthy, and the company is profitable. Instead, put yourself in Mark Watney's dire circumstances. Force yourself to think differently. By doing so you will create a better strategy, one that reduces the chance that the Wheel of Fortune will deal you misfortune.

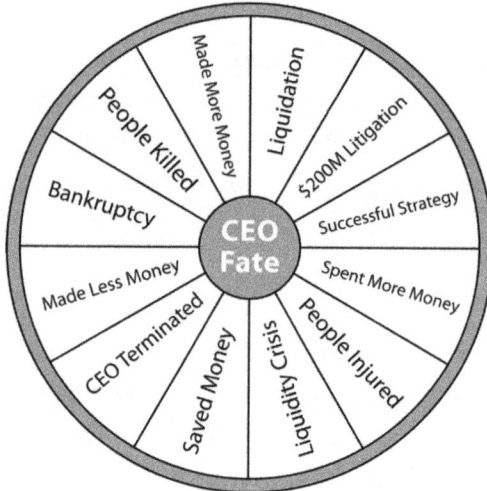

To be focused on success is to be unprepared for misfortune.

Notes

1. The strategy failures that Emiliani and his students have analyzed over the years indicate that the processes most leaders use to create strategy, while perhaps structured and likely elaborate in varied forms of analysis, are rife with defects that often combine to produce damaging or catastrophic results. It is further likely that analyses are sometimes made to fit the leaders' desired strategy, thus assuring that defects are built into the strategy and remain hidden.

2. There is an obvious incongruity between leaders' desire to maintain the status quo and the continuously changing circumstances in which business must operate – even if it attains sacred monopoly status. While leaders often implore employees to avoid complacency, take fast action, and the like, the same cannot generally be said for senior leaders who most often remain stuck in their ways (see Chapter 1, Reference 3). Being leaders, they have the right and privilege to do that, though others have no choice but to bear the consequences. This inculcates future leaders, from one generation to the next, to believe they can and should do the same. It is a pernicious disabling of needed progress.

3. Requiring people or teams to argue both sides, for and against, focused questions are beneficial in these six ways: It facilitates a deeper exploration of ideas, challenge people's thinking, raises the level of intellectual discourse, allows people to step outside of groupthink bubbles, learn from each other, and develop themselves.

References

[1] Weir, A. (2014), *The Martian*, Broadway Books, New York, New York

[2] Isaacson, W. (2017), *Leonardo da Vinci*, Simon & Schuster, New York, New York

[3] Clinton, C. (2005), *Harriet Tubman: The Road to Freedom*, Back Bay Books, New York, New York

[4] Curie, E. (2001), *Madame Curie: A Biography*, De Capo Press, Cambridge, Massachusetts

Final Thoughts

Final Thoughts

Wheel of Fortune contains a potentially conflicting message: strategy is necessary, yet perhaps it is not necessary. Strategy is necessary because it can provide focus and direction to many people, aid in decision-making, help allocate resources, and so on. Strategy may be unnecessary because of its high failure rate and the embarrassing and costly misfortune that results from it. Perhaps it is better to simply focus on execution at all levels. But execution is not a strategy. It is a platitude like "we put customers first" or slogan-as-strategy such as "do it all." Execution it is merely doing what professionals should do in the competent planning and performance of their duties and tasks. Too often people, starting with senior leaders, make mistakes characteristic of amateur levels of skill, not professional levels of skill. So, executing one's work, again, at all levels, should follow the model that anyone who claims to be a professional uses – the Plan, Do, Study, Adjust (PDSA) cycle (see Note 1). Does that obviate the need for business strategy? Perhaps not. But a business that executes professionally, with few mistakes, will likely come out ahead of one that has a strategy (good or bad) that executes poorly and with many errors.

If business leaders are set on the idea that strategy is necessary, it is almost certainly tied to an overarching goal of pecuniary gain, often characterized by "the growth imperative" (Table 1-1). This brings related phrases to mind such as "if you're not growing, you are going backwards" and "grow or die." Do leaders ever test the truth of these statements?

- Is it really true that if you don't grow the company will die, or if the company is not growing it is going backwards?
- Why is growth so important to a company?
- Who is asking the company to grow? Customers, employees, suppliers, investors, communities, competitors?

Most competitors do not like it when a company grows because it creates more work for leaders. Communities like it when companies grow because it usually means more jobs for its residents. Investors explicitly ask for companies to grow so they can increase their wealth. Suppliers like it when their customers grow because it can mean more sales, though, unfortunately, they may get beaten down in prices. Most employees like it when the company grows because it can mean higher pay, better benefits, and new opportunities. Customers? They do not ask companies to grow. Most dislike it when a company grows because it often means higher prices, less choice, and a diminution in quality, service, or other features that they value, driven by management's pursuit of pecuniary gain at their expense. While some stakeholders have interest or disinterest in growth, growth is clearly driven most by the narrow desires of a special interest group, investors, who view business as little more than a financial instrument. As such, it is trivial to state why growth is seen as being so important:

- Makes a company more valuable
- The company generates more cash
- Increases shareholder value

- Get a higher price when the property is sold
- Allows the company to borrow more money at lower rates
- Company is harder to take over because it is more expensive to buy

But it is not trivial to recite the many downsides of growth that are often dismissed by senior leaders:

- Hide systemic and day-to-day problems
- Sacrifice the future for short-term gains
- Ignore diseconomies of scale
- Diversification into lines of business whose risks are poorly understood
- Difficulty digesting acquisitions, realizing synergies, and harmonizing corporate cultures
- Game financial and other performance metrics to achieve the appearance of growth
- Reduced competition and customer choice
- Focus becomes on getting people to buy things they do not need (increase SG&A costs)
- Trains people to do things required to grow sales, which develops the wrong skill set for when decline inevitably comes
- Increased leverage (reduced safety factor)
- Leadership and management complacency

And because the downsides of growth, particularly high (double digit) growth, are normally dismissed by success-oriented leaders, business strategy takes on additional risk which increases the probability of failure. When that happens, senior leaders again turn to the CEOs Wealth Creation Playbook (Table 1-1), just as they would do if they had no formalized business strategy. So, what does business strategy accomplish, other than satisfying an obligatory social requirement for those who are high in status, much in the same way expensive clothes, cars, watches, and homes do? In most cases, strategy is more decorative than functional.

If the intent for business strategy is to be functional, then structured problems-solving coupled with creative and innovative thinking is required to avoid disasters as large as the Boeing 737 Max or smaller calamities that somehow harm customers, employees, or suppliers – all of which harm investors and communities, but which give welcome relief to competitors. Merely copying the strategy of others is intrinsically inadequate given leaders' roles and responsibilities, and because what is copied was likely not to be the result of good thinking. Clearly, the work of developing strategy must be professionalized to avoid embedding mistakes into it and reduce the errors that can occur in execution.

• • • •

This book has sought to analyze business strategy from a direction that is substantially different from others. Facing these facts is surely discomforting because the mirror does not deceive. It reflects the truth and offers a choice: Strategies that lead to a closing-off of competition or improving competitive strength and vitality by reimagining the business ecosystem. These choices embody different sets of practical values that manifest themselves as a march towards monopoly or the flowering of competition.

Traditional ways of thinking, rooted in archaic preconceptions, concentrate risk such that strategy can backfire in spectacular and tragic ways. The larger the company, the more likely it is that leaders, far from the actual work, inadvertently build excessive risk into their strategy. In effect, leaders are unable to differentiate between good strategy and destructive strategy. Either form of strategy can fool leaders given the likely precision of analysis that went into formulating the strategy, which produces overconfidence in both the merits of the strategy and the ease with which it can be executed.

In contrast, reimagining the need for and consequence of business strategy can reduce corporate clutter and distribute risk more widely. This dilution of risk produces a more natural commercial environment that expands choices and establishes conditions by which human talent and creativity can more freely flourish. This raises the potential for constructive expression and human satisfaction throughout the hierarchy.

The need for and construction of strategy is driven by the social requirements of business leadership and the exigencies of business. It is the former that leads to the embedding of mistakes in strategy that come to fruition as execution unfolds over time. Senior leaders should never think that their beliefs and untested assumptions are sound, that they are free of cognitive biases, and that they are immune to illogical thinking. The greater one's success, the more likely these are to plague strategy and decision-making. Leaders' instinct or propensity for exploit, seizure, cunning, and prowess and associated gamesmanship virtually assures that strategy will be embedded with many defects.

On the one hand there are continuous formal or informal efforts to develop leadership competencies in the face of competition, yet on the other hand there can be a continuous undoing of leadership competencies caused by the pursuit of pecuniary gain resulting from the march toward monopoly. Rather than accepting the ever-changing nature of business and improving leadership and organizational adaptive capabilities, the typical response is to do what has been done in the past. Whether through copying others' strategy or business-as-usual in terms of leadership and management practice, the work of leadership does little more than meet minimum requirements. Leaders' disdain for workers and their labor is mirrored in their dislike of the mental work that is required of them to assure that the company can effectively compete in the marketplace over extended periods of time.

Wheel of Fortune has ventured to show there are serious gaps in senior leadership skills and capabilities that, if corrected, will improve and professionalize the work of leading and managing organizations. The social science of strategy describes how mistakes become embedded in strategy. The

Strategy Failure Analysis Method illuminates and magnifies the varied types of mistakes so that corrections can be made. The Strategy Acid Test allows for proactive identification of mistakes and corrections prior to strategy execution. The structured problems-solving method, integrated with the Strategy Acid Test offers a pathway for formulating better strategies, if there is a need for strategy. This mental model compels a better understanding business strategy such that old, recurring problems can be solved with new thinking driven by imagination and creativity. Senior leaders who are able to change their mind can create the conditions for designing a strategy that is both original and which has lower risk of failure.

The COVID-19 pandemic, the poor response from most leaders, and the 2008 economic crisis that has never been resolved, unfortunately demonstrate how much it is necessary to rethink various ways of business and the need for creating new directions and improving existing paths. Everything begins with the observation of situations and how we think about problems and solutions, starting with our assumptions and preconceptions that guide and influence our thinking. The difficulty of thinking differently lies behind many of the problems that afflict leaders and organizations. And that is where change must start.

Notes

1. Professionals in diverse field may not know the PDSA cycle, but that is essentially what they are doing as they seek to gain mastery in their given field. If business activities at all levels were executed as deftly as professional athletes or musicians do their work, making very few errors, then it might outrun the need for repetitive cycles of (good or bad) strategy formulation and execution that have high risks of falling short of expectations or failing. To grasp the scope and multitude of errors that leaders make, see Emiliani, B. (2015), *Speed Leadership: A New Way to Lead for Rapidly Changing Times*, The CLBM, LLC Wethersfield, Connecticut

Worksheets

What Did You Learn?

Sketch or write some key learnings from this book.

Preface

Introduction

Chapter 1 – Business and Strategy

Chapter 2 – Social Science of Strategy

Chapter 3 – Strategy Failure Analysis

Chapter 4 – Strategic Choices: Copy or Create

Chapter 5 – Imagination and Creativity

Final Thoughts

What Final Thoughts Do You Have?

What Key Learnings From This Book Will You Share with the Senior Leadership Team?

-

-

-

-

-

-

What Will You Change or Do Differently Based on What You Learned from This Book?

•

•

•

•

•

•

What Must You Do to Make This Happen?

Actions to Take	By When	Person Responsible

What Types of Resistance Do You Expect to Encounter?

-
-
-
-
-
-

What Must You Do to Gain Support?

-
-
-
-
-

About the Authors

M.L. "Bob" Emiliani is a professor in the School of Engineering, Science, and Technology at Connecticut State University in New Britain, Connecticut, where he teaches a course on leadership, a unique course that analyzes failures in management decision-making, as well as other courses.

Bob earned a Bachelor of Science degree in mechanical engineering from the University of Miami, a Master of Science degree in chemical engineering from the University of Rhode Island, and a Doctor of Philosophy degree in Engineering from Brown University.

He worked in the consumer products and aerospace industries for 15 years, beginning as a materials engineer. He has held management positions in engineering, manufacturing, and supply chain management at Pratt & Whitney.

Bob joined academia in September 1999. While in academia, he developed the Lean teaching pedagogy and led activities to continuously improve master's degree programs.

Emiliani has authored or co-authored 24 books, four book chapters, and more than 45 peer-reviewed papers. He has received six awards for writing.

Please visit www.bobemiliani.com
LinkedIn @Bob Emiliani

About the Authors

Massimo Torinesi worked for twenty years at Esselte, a leading worldwide manufacturer of office supplies, where he held positions of increasing responsibility in operations. His last position at Esselte was Operations Director for three manufacturing plants. He was also in charge of process improvement in collaboration with leading Japanese and American consultants.

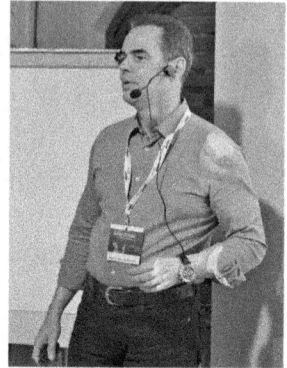

In 2007 Massimo joined a global consulting company as a senior consultant working with numerous international businesses to help them understand and implement the kaizen philosophy.

Massimo later co-founded his own company, Heiko Xplore, in Milan, Italy. Through the years he has led over 700 workshops focused on business design. He is a creative, blogger, and keynote speaker. Massimo facilitates leadership teams to improve strategy, operations, product development, and sales and marketing. He teaches clients how to achieve sustainable long-term growth by following three paths: 1) operational excellence; 2) innovation, and, most importantly, 3) engaging people at all levels in organizations. To support these three paths, Massimo continuously develops new approaches to leadership. He is the author or co-author of two books.

Please visit www.heikoxplore.com
LinkedIn @Massimo Torinesi
Instagram @massimo.torinesi

www.ingramcontent.com/pod-product-compliance
Lightning Source LLC
Chambersburg PA
CBHW031811190326
41518CB00006B/287